AF498611

How to Make People Like You

19 Effortless Ways to Boost Your Personality, Attract More People, and Make Friends Scientifically (2022 Guide for Beginners)

Daisy Byrd

Contents

NTRODUCTION

"The most beautiful thing you can have is confidence." – Sabrina Carpenter.

Consider yourself back in school. Take a moment to reflect on how you felt at the time. I'm talking about when you're 13 or 14, just entering your adolescent years.

You come and go from school. During breaks, you sit in on lessons and play games. You collaborate with classmates on group projects and study for essays and exams. You meet your first love, your first girlfriend or boyfriend, and spend your weekends running around with your friends.

As you grew older, you began to form your own social circles. You may have remained friends with people from your childhood, or as you progressed through higher education, college, and university, you began to mix with new groups of friends. People arrived and left.

As you learned more about yourself and what you liked and didn't like, you began to meet new people who shared your interests.

Whether you liked going out and partying, reading, hanging out, watching movies, playing video games, or watching sports, there were always people you could call your friends. Maybe you're still friends with some of those people, or maybe you've gone your separate ways in life.

I've been thinking about this journey of friendships that we have all taken over the last few years. I'm aware that some people had a difficult childhood. Children can be cruel, and things like bullying can make some of them feel like outcasts. But even back then, I remember kids in my school who were bullied by some of their classmates, but they still had a group of friends to call their own.

My illness was social anxiety. It wasn't too bad in school, but it became more noticeable as I approached my adolescence and then college. I just discovered that I couldn't talk to anyone or form new relationships. I had a few friends from school with whom I kept in touch on occasion, but it was extremely difficult for me to meet and connect with new people.

I just couldn't seem to pull it off.

My self-esteem had plummeted, and this had harmed my belief in myself. It felt like I was trapped in a vicious cycle of not being able to talk to people, feeling anxious about it, and then feeling even more anxious about not being able to talk to others. It was impeding my progress in life.

It wasn't until my twenties, when I landed my first "real" job in sales and marketing that I realized this was a problem that was holding me back. Because you're reading this book right now, you're probably already aware of what I'm referring to.

That feeling of reflecting on your childhood and wondering how you made friends so easily and how you were able to talk to people without being shy or overthinking every interaction. That awe-inspiring feeling of having so many friends and acquaintances when you were younger, but now you only have a handful of friends, some of whom you only speak to once in a blue moon.

Don't worry; you're not alone in your thoughts.

The Age of Connectivity

We are all living in the modern human era's new, unprecedented hyper-connected world. Social media, for example, has taken over and become an absolute necessity in our daily lives. Human connection is undergoing a transformation unprecedented in the history of the human race.

According to 2019 statistics, 61 percent of Americans admit to having regular feelings of loneliness, up 7 percent from the previous year, and 52 percent feel lonely "most of the time" or "always." According to a similar YouGov poll conducted in 2019, 21 percent of Americans have "no close friends," and 58 percent feel that no one knows them well. As you can probably guess from these statistics, 53 percent of people find it difficult to make friends.

These statistics are mirrored in nearly every Western country, including the majority of the EU, the United Kingdom, Mexico, Japan, Greece, Israel, and many others. This isn't just happening in isolated areas of the world; it's happening everywhere.

These are a slew of eye-opening statistics, some of which will no doubt surprise you, but they paint a clear picture. We are all becoming more disconnected from one another, and the longer this disconnect persists, the more difficult it appears to be to reconnect. When you consider the isolating nature of society, politics, gender, and race discussions and the massive impact of the 2020 COVID-19 pandemic, these are issues that will cause an increasing number of problems on a large scale.

But I don't want to get into the large-scale consequences of this loneliness epidemic. It gives the impression that everything is doom and gloom, which is not the case. It may appear simple, but you must scale everything back and examine your relationships and ability to connect in your own life. You must concentrate on the small, personal scale.

Once you're here, you can begin learning about how your mind works and what's going on within you that causes you to disconnect from others or why you're having difficulty connecting with new people. You can then use this information as a foundation to learn new techniques for cultivating vibrant and exciting relationships, as well as new skills for meeting and conversing with new people, even total strangers.

You give yourself the opportunity to form new friendships, which you then develop into friendships that will last for years. You learn how to reconnect, which is exactly what we'll be doing throughout this book.

It's a New Day. A Fresh Start

I spent the majority of my early and mid-twenties stuck in a rut due to social anxiety. I was an outcast who felt lonely almost every day. I was that guy in the background at work who you probably knew my name or saw at the Christmas party once or twice but don't remember ever talking to. My cheeks are flushing and getting hot just thinking about it.

When I was about 28 years old, I decided enough was enough. There has to be a better way to live. I must be able to learn how to communicate with others. I recall one day when there was a promotion for a manager position in my sales firm. I was the lead project manager for a new client we were taking on, and it was one of those opportunities that was tailor-made for me. I knew if I got the job, I'd be fantastic at it. It would be my opportunity to shine.

Unfortunately, I never dared to speak up, and even during my interview, my boss stated that I was good, but not the people person they were looking for.

Do you know who was hired?

Everyone greeted the confident, charismatic guy who walked into the office, and even the postman who came in would stop to chat with him. I used to be so envious of how he carried himself. It wasn't even conceited or egotistical. You were drawn in by his natural charm and charisma. He was genuine, and even if you had nothing in common, you wanted to talk to him and hear what he had to say.

I'm not a big believer in auras or spiritual connections, but he was one of those guys who walked into a room and everyone felt his presence. I'm sure you know people like this in your life.

It took a few years and a lot of practice to realize that you can become like this person, but not exactly this person.

You have the ability to become your own person. You can become the authentic, unadulterated, unfiltered, genuine, and connection-worthy version of yourself. As with anything else in life, all it takes is a little know-how, practice, and a willingness to consider what is possible.

Allow yourself to open your mind to this new way of being right now.

If you can't, take that last sentence as my permission to broaden your horizons. I'm going to detail everything I've learned on my journey in the following pages of this book so you can increase your charisma, spark attraction in the people in your life, win friends, nurture and build relationships, attract romantic partners, and connect with other human beings in ways you've never connected with them before.

After a lot of self-reflection, I've narrowed everything down to just 19 easy-to-follow methods, backed up by scientific research, and complete with everything you need to know about making friends in the modern age. Every single method in this book is actionable right now, and by the time you're finished reading it, you'll feel better about yourself in ways you won't believe.

And with that, I'm sure you've had enough of me, and you're eager to get started, so follow me down the rabbit hole, keep your hands and feet inside the carriage at all times, and let's get started learning.

Part One
The Beginning of Something New

"Strangers are just waiting to become friends." – Mckuen, Rod

Every single relationship that has does, or will ever exist begins the same way: with one person talking to another. To start a relationship, you must first meet people and make that first connection.

It makes no difference what kinds of relationships you want in your life or what kinds of relationships you're reading this book to attract.

First impressions are always the most important, and you must be able to talk to new people, make them like you right away, and even have the confidence to make this all happen in the first place.

This is why I'm starting here. Throughout the following chapters (which I'll refer to as methods), we'll look at some of the best ways to gain confidence in meeting and talking to new people, starting conversations, and generally getting your foot in the door when it comes to connecting with others.

Method 1
It's All About the Smile

"When you smile, the rest of the world smiles with you."-Louis Armstrong

When Louis Armstrong, one of the most famous jazz musicians of all time, sang these words for the first time, he probably had no idea that scientific studies would one day back up his claim.

You probably already know this and have experienced it numerous times throughout your life, which is why it is my first and foremost method for cultivating beautiful relationships with others. It is literally centered on one action.

Smiling.

Smiling is such a powerful action, both physically and subconsciously. Smiling is a universal human trait, which means that it doesn't matter what culture you're in or who you're talking to; smiling makes us all feel the same. It's natural for us to react this way when we see someone smiling.

Best of all, this has been proven time and again, through personal experiences as well as scientific studies.

A 2002 Swedish study on body language, mimicry, and emotional empathy discovered that people who were shown images of other people smiling found it "incredibly difficult" to frown or display traditionally negative emotions. They actually went a step further and discovered that doing anything other than smiling when you see someone else smiling requires a conscious effort.

That's how natural it is to smile.

Of course, smiling is a very positive emotion that makes you feel good. When it comes to forming relationships and friendships with others, you want them to see you in a positive light, which is why smiling is such an effective method of attracting others. Consider the last time you saw someone at work crying, sad, or extremely angry. What are you going to do?

So, if you're like most people, or at least like me, you'll be very unsure about how to proceed. Do you communicate with them?

Can you assist them? Attempt to make them laugh? Leave them alone for a while? These kinds of emotions are fraught with uncertainty, and anyone who experiences them is left feeling unsure.

On the other hand, if you walk into work and see someone smiling, nodding, or even just smiling at their computer, the situation feels stable and secure. You can talk to that person, and if anything, you want to talk to them even more because they're smiling. As you read this, I'm sure you're picturing situations in your life where this has occurred, or at least you are right now!

Consider a restaurant where the waitress greeted you with a huge smile before showing you to your table and how welcomed you felt. Compare that to the grunt from the other restaurant waiter, who was clearly having a bad day and made you feel uneasy. I'm sure you see what I'm saying.

Your smile alters how you see the world

As well as how others perceive it.

In a 2015 study published in "Social Cognitive and Affective Neuroscience," researchers conducted some very interesting research on this topic. They discovered in their research that the act of smiling or seeing someone else smile physically alters our emotions and feelings. They discovered this by actively monitoring the electrical activity in their volunteers' brains. What were the outcomes?

When people smiled at the volunteers, it immediately made them feel better. They conducted numerous tests, and as a result of this research, they discovered that when humans see what is known as a "neutral" face, they automatically assume that person is feeling neutral. Are there any surprises in there?

However, when you see someone smiling, you automatically assume that person is "happy." When it comes to making new friends and connecting with people, this is a crucial factor to consider. By smiling, you spread positive energy to those around you. This encourages them to approach you, connect with you, and simply be in your presence more. Simply walking into a room and smiling is an excellent way to initiate a conversation and pique people's interest in what you have to say.

Similarly, when you smile, your brain releases feel-good chemicals called serotonin, which make you feel good. Do you not believe me? Attempt it right now. Look away from the book and out a window, towards someone you care about, a pet, a stranger, a tree, or anything else that comes to mind. Simply smile now. Even if you're not in the mood to smile, give it a shot.

I'll wait a second.

Even now, as I write this, I can't help but laugh to myself as I push air out of my nose. That is the power that a smile has. Even if you're having the worst day you can imagine, taking a few moments to smile and be present is enough to put you in a good mood. And, as research has repeatedly shown, this positive effect spreads to those around you.

Never underestimate the effectiveness of a smile.

Action Item: Smiling More!

Given that this is the first chapter, I'll keep the takeaway simple and something you can start working on right away. Consider this your homework, but you will not receive a grade at the end. Instead, you have the opportunity to form more meaningful relationships and connect with people who come and go in your life much more easily.

Here's what you should do.

Ready?

All you need to do is smile more!

That's all there is to it. I know it sounds simple, and you probably guessed that was what I was going to say anyway, but, and I'll say it one more time to emphasize this point, you should never underestimate the power of a smile.

Give it a shot. Talk to the cashier the next time you go into a store, pass someone on the street, talk to someone at work, or see your partner when you get home. Grin at them. Say hello and put on your best smile for them. If you're meeting a new customer, make a conscious effort to smile at them and make yourself as appealing as possible.

The results speak for themselves, so give it a shot and become your own proof. Now, I know this method is very simple, and you've probably heard something similar before, but you'd be surprised how few people realize how effective it is. If you can't bring yourself to smile, you could always consider getting a dog.

People are always happy when they see a dog.

Anyway, all jokes aside, simply smiling more isn't the only way to make friends and become more approachable. This, however, is only the tip of the iceberg. Let's take a look at some other approaches that can help you achieve your connection objectives.

Method 2
Always Be the First to Act

"You can't stay in your Forest corner and wait for others to come to you. You must visit them on occasion." A. Milne, Winnie-the-Pooh Pooh

Consider this.

You could board a bus or a train and discover that the person sitting next to you is someone you were destined to be best friends with. You may share a lot of interests, musical tastes, and a love of classic movies. It's effortless that you \stwo would share many great experiences and could spend an entire \slifetime having fun, making memories, and enjoying life in so many \samazing ways.

There is, however, a catch. One of you must first speak to the other.

It breaks my heart that we live in such a secluded and closed-off world, isolating ourselves from one another.

Hey, I've been on both sides of the fence. I've been the closed-off person who sits on the train and does everything in my power to avoid acknowledging existence from everyone else. I've also been the guy who sits back and watches everyone else be that person.

We live in a world where people are afraid to speak to one another. We're even afraid to look each other in the eyes for more than a split second. Instead, we retreat into our comfort zones, scroll endlessly through social media feeds we don't genuinely care about, plug in our headphones, and shut ourselves off from the world and any potential interaction. After all, imagine talking to someone and having their advances or conversation efforts rejected!

Would you be able to handle that kind of rejection?

Well, I've always assumed the answer was no. It was too much for me to bear. I remember being in college and seeing a beautiful girl in the same course but in a different class. I adored her in every way. Her tone of voice.Her command of the English language. I was completely smitten in a way I'd never felt before. But did I ever speak to her? No way, no how.

I lacked the confidence to make the first move. And who knows, maybe she wasn't brave enough to make the first move with me, but she felt the same way I did. In this case, you have two people who want to have a deep and meaningful connection with each other. Neither of them, however, has the courage to say hello. Doesn't that seem ridiculous when you think about it from a birds-eye perspective?

My friend was the polar opposite. He was a big fan of the computer game League of Legends a few years ago. You play with five other people on your team and can choose to play with friends or strangers on the internet. He played with someone, and they did well, winning several games in a row.

They would communicate via voice chat while playing, and it turned out that the player was a girl. They eventually exchanged phone numbers, added each other on social media, and dated for more than a year.

Isn't that insane? The chances of them being paired together, logging onto the computer game at precisely the right time to be paired up, out of 160 million other global players, are practically nil.

But they were able to enjoy each other's company and have such a beautiful relationship. They're no longer together due to difficult mental health issues that were getting in the way, but they're still very close friends who chat every week and play together on occasion. Isn't that lovely?

These two people enjoyed each other's company because one of them initiated the relationship, allowing it to blossom into something wonderful that they both share. This brings me nicely to method number two: always be the first to make a move.

The Science for Taking the First Step

As human beings, we're conditioned to fear rejection. We're social animals, and it's in our million-year-old instinct to stay a part of the pack. Human beings couldn't survive on their own. If you're wandering around the wildernesses of 1000 BC and you get sick or injure yourself, then chances are you're going to die. On the other hand, if you have your tribe around you, they can look after you, and you can look after them (more on this reciprocation nature later, by the way!). You're more likely to survive.

However, as time has progressed and we no longer live in tribes of 50 people or so, but instead have the ability to connect with literally millions of people across the internet, all judging and criticizing everything all the time, we're trained ourselves to hate rejection. In fact, we do everything we can to not risk being rejected at all, and that means we stop ourselves from taking that first, potentially embarrassing, and painful step.

If I had spoken to the girl I fancied at college and said, "Hey, want to get to know each other? I think you're cute," and she went "Urgh, get away from me, loser!" then yeah, I'm probably going to feel a little crushed. But, time being the best medicine, I would eventually get over it. Sure, the experience would then tell me not to do it again because 100 percent of the time I had been crushed, but think about how many friends you have had in your life.

You've spoken to them all for the first time at one point, so it's safe to say rejection doesn't happen all the time. As human beings are once more conditioned, we always remember the negative things that happen far more than we do the positives, which is why you need to consciously spend effort in thinking positively. This is another great reason why you should practice smiling to yourself more; to think more positively!

So, going back to taking the first step. Everyone is afraid of taking the first step, but in almost all situations, if you can do it, then you've taken the risk off of that other person, put them at ease, and now that first barrier is out of the way, you can start building your relationship with them.

Psychologists Steven Asher and Sherri Oden carried out a study that proves this to be the case. They studied elementary school children to see how they made friends with other children and how they were accepted, thus overcoming the fear of rejection.

They discovered one of the most important and essential skills a child needs to have when trying to make new friends and form new relationships is the ability to initiate an engagement—aka, taking that first step in communicating with another human being.

In this study, sure, the kids were inviting other kids to come and play in the fort castle or wanted to see if the other girl wanted to come and play with the same doll. If you have kids or have been around children, then you know that they'll do this. They'll bring over a toy to someone and see if you want to play together, and this is the foundation for the new relationship.

Of course, I'm not saying you need to invite your work colleagues over to play in a pillow fort together (some workplaces have rules against that kind of behavior), but there are more adult ways of taking that first step.

Action Time – Take the First Step

I know what you're thinking, and I understand. It's hard to take the first step because you need a certain degree of confidence, and the pressures of being rejected can leave you feeling absolutely crushed, sometimes even paralyzed. I know. I've been there myself, and you may truly believe there's no other way to be.

I'm going to talk more about being confident and ways to boost this way of thinking in future chapters, but I want you to start small for now. By starting small, you can build up your confidence over time with little wins, and then this kind of personal development will really start to snowball. This is how it worked for me, as I'm sure it can work for you too.

When I say starting small, I mean to make the first move in small situations. This could be talking to the cashier in the shop. It only has to be small talk, but use the opportunity to practice. You can speak to the people around you in a queue, people at work, and even the people you live with. Keep building up your confidence and having these small interactions, and soon you'll be able to talk to anyone about anything, right from the time you meet them.

Over time, you'll get better and better at doing this, which will lead to the confidence you need to make deep, meaningful relationships and come across as the most confident, charismatic version of yourself possible. However, this isn't the only way to start a relationship.

There's one more I want to talk about before moving on.

Method 3
Excuse Me. Can You Help Me?

"The power of asking is the key to abundance living." – Lailah Gifty Akita

There are a few things to think about when it comes to connecting with other people. You need trust on both sides. You need confidence. You must be able to speak up, make the first move, and establish some sort of connection that will lead to friendship and beyond. While it may seem counterintuitive, asking someone for a favor is one of the most effective ways to accomplish this psychologically.

Obviously, I'm not suggesting that you sit next to someone on the train, strike up a conversation with them, and then invite them to stay in your home to look after your dog. There are obviously big and small favors, but asking for a favor can be a great way to begin and develop a relationship with someone.

Please allow me to explain.

When you ask someone for a favor, you're not just asking for assistance from someone; you're specifically asking the person you're asking. Assume you're at work and starting a new project for a new client. You have some ideas, but you're not sure which path to take. What are you going to do?

You could, for example, ask a coworker for advice or a suggestion. This is not only a sign of intimacy, but it is also a sign of trust. You're telling the other person, "Hey, I respect you and your opinion, and I trust your judgment on this subject." Can you share some of your knowledge with me? Obviously, you're not saying this aloud, but the fact that you're asking for it suggests that this is how you feel. After all, you're not going to ask someone for their opinion if you're not interested in that other person or their thoughts.

This means you've already laid the groundwork for a friendship, and if people believe you like them (because you're not going to ask for a favor if you don't), they'll already have a positive attitude toward you. This, in turn, leads to another connection, and so on.

According to a Harvard study titled "Very Happy People," there is a 0.7 correlation between people who give social support and their happiness. This means that the more people who help others and give rather than take, the happier they are. As an example, a 0.7 correlation is greater than the one between smoking and cancer.

This is why people marry. Because you're sharing your life, you're there for each other through thick and thin. You assist each other with daily tasks, encourage each other to live your best lives, and are generally there for each other when you need them.

Making Others Feel Good

When it comes to relationships, the advantages of asking for help are limitless. According to a human relations study conducted by Jon Decker, asking for a favor boosts the other person's self-esteem, and as a result, they will like you more.

We are hardwired as humans to want to belong to a group of other people. We are social beings. No one wants to be an outcast from the group, and everyone wants to be accepted. Acceptance of what they can bring to the table, both in terms of actions and ideas, is part of this. Because you're ticking all the boxes, it's as if you're tapping into this area of the mind by asking for favors.

You want the people you ask for favors to feel safe and as if they belong.

You're agreeing to them.

It also makes people feel capable because you're asking them to do something because you believe they're capable of doing it. This is a significant boost to their self-esteem and self-confidence, which comes from you, and it increases how much of a positive light they see you in.

All of these are necessary for making friends and making people feel good about themselves.

Action Time – Requesting Small, Appropriate Favors

So, now that we've discussed why asking for favors can be a great way to connect with others, it's time to put it all into practice. As I mentioned in the beginning of this chapter, you're not going to ask a complete stranger to look after your house for you, so start with small favors appropriate for the people you're talking to.

For example, if you need assistance moving or a ride to the airport, you could ask a coworker. Thank them, and perhaps bring them something to thank them for from your vacation, and the favor is done.

However, while this is, in essence, a quick favor, this interaction can do so much for building up your relationship with that person.

Another example we've already discussed is soliciting ideas from others.

Whether you're working on a project at work, looking for vacation ideas, need a package picked up, or need a lift somewhere, these are all acceptable reasons to ask someone you don't know very well.

As your relationships become more trustworthy and meaningful, you can begin to ask for more favors, such as babysitting your child or looking after a pet for the weekend. Don't confuse this with having to ask for favors all the time, even if you don't need them. If you're only asking for favors because you can, you're not being genuine, and it's not the best way to start a new relationship.

If you need assistance with something or want to welcome someone new into your life by making them feel welcomed, accepted, and appreciated, this is the best method to use every time. That brings us to the end of Part One! So far, what are your thoughts? Have you discovered any effective ways to begin conversing with others? This is, of course, the first step to being the charismatic and confident version of yourself, so make sure you get creative with how you use these methods and keep practicing them!

Furthermore, and perhaps more excitingly, we're now moving into part two, where we'll focus on a few of the methods you can use to deepen your connection with someone once you've begun to get to know them. It's all about how you can take any level of relationship and transform it into a deep and meaningful one.

Part Two
Planting the Seeds of Something Lovely

This chapter's phrasing is perfect: "sowing the seeds for something beautiful." I know I wrote it, but when you think about it in terms of a relationship, it conjures up images in your mind of what a relationship in your own life could look like. It could be a friendship, a romantic relationship, a parent-child relationship, or even a professional relationship.

Every relationship has the potential to be beautiful in its own unique way.

However, you must first arrive. When I first started dating and was working on overcoming my social anxiety, I spent a lot of time dealing with the issues we discussed in Part One. When I met people, I was gaining confidence and making the first move. This was especially noticeable in my dating life. That was fine because I was working on being able to talk to girls and ask them out on dates. It took some practice, but I eventually got there.

Then there was the date, which was a whole different ballgame.

There's a big difference between meeting someone for the first time and meeting them again, getting to know them, and moving forward. This section will be covered in the next five chapters. We'll look at five powerful techniques that can help you build relationships, improve your charisma, make friends, and deepen your connections with others.

Method 4
Improving Your Listening Skills

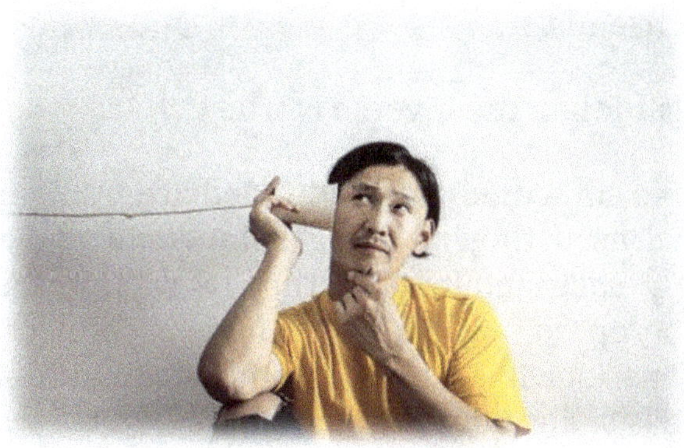

"When people speak, pay close attention." Most people never listen." -Ernest Hemingway

You've probably heard this before, but being able to listen to someone is one of the most important skills you can have when it comes to connecting with them. I'm sure you've been in a situation where you've been talking to someone about something you're passionate about, but you don't feel like they're listening.

Maybe they're on their phone, staring out the window, or everything about them, including their body language, says they don't care. I'm sure you can think of times when you did something similar or someone you know who did something similar. Take a moment to think about how this feels.

What are your thoughts? Do you have a sad feeling? Pushed aside? Ignored?

Unaccepted? As if what you have to say isn't good enough or worthwhile of their time? Whatever you're feeling, it's not a good feeling, and not listening to people and making them feel this way isn't going to win you any friends.

Having said that, the inverse is true.

If you give someone your undivided attention and make them feel as if they're being listened to and that you genuinely care about what they're saying, they'll feel happy, accepted, and as if you have a connection with them. This is why, when it comes to making friends, listening is so important.

Carl Rogers, a well-known American psychologist, famously stated that active and deep listening is the foundation of any healthy relationship. You can encourage strength and growth in any relationship by mastering the art of listening, and people who are heard are less likely to be defensive and more open to new ideas.

This means that listening to them will not only make them happier and more connected to you, but it will also increase the likelihood that they will listen to you. This is how a healthy, two-way relationship develops.

There Are Two Kinds of Listening

Faye Doell's 2003 study discovered two main types of listening a person can do, three if you count not actually listening but pretending to. You're doing one of two things if you're actively listening to someone speak. You're either A listening to understand the other person or B listening to respond to them.

How many times have you been in a conversation and known what you're going to say before the other person has finished speaking? Yes, I'm sure we've all done it at some point. This usually happens in heated debates or arguments where you may not agree with what someone is saying, and they say their point, and you respond with something like "Yeah, but...", and then you go straight into your point.

This is listening to respond because you're not really listening; instead, you're waiting for the other person to finish so you can speak.

This will not make the other person feel heard, and your relationship will suffer as a result.

On the other hand, if you listen to understand, you are truly listening to what the other person is saying and how they feel. Based on what they say, you formulate a response that advances the conversation, whether you ask a question to better understand what they're saying or you accept what they're saying and then bring up a counterpoint.

According to the same studies, people who listen to understand have much greater and more satisfying relationships. Assume you're the type of person who wants to "fix" other people, with good intentions. In that case, you're probably listening to respond most of the time because you're flexing your desire to influence others, which leads to you not actually listening to the other, but again, listening to respond.

To make a long story short, if you want better, more satisfying relationships in which you are properly listened to and are happier with the people you are connected with, you must learn how to listen to understand.

Time for Action – How to Become a Better Listener

While many of us, including you, have bad habits when it comes to listening to others, everyone can improve their listening skills by focusing on a few key points. The more you practice these points, the better you'll become and, as a result, the better your relationships will be. Let's get started.

Feelings for the Speaker

The first, and always a great way to instantly become a better listener, is to put yourself in the mind of the person you're listening to.

Take on the role of the one who is speaking. Because you can resonate with and understand what is being said, this can bring a lot more compassion and empathy into your conversations.

Let's say someone comes to talk to you because they've had a bad day at work. They made a mistake on a project and are afraid of being fired. You could listen to respond and have all these ideas on how to make things better, or they could redeem their mistake or offer advice on how to accept the situation they're in.

On the other hand, you can listen to understand and feel that yes, they are concerned, and while they believe they may be fired, you can ask further questions to see if that is likely, or what they believe they can do to make things better. This is listening to understand, and approaching a situation in this manner is far more beneficial.

Along with this, you should consider the meaning of what the person is saying. This can be obvious at times and subtle at others, but listening for the meaning behind why someone is saying something will help you understand them tenfold.

You'll be able to identify what someone is saying to you if you pay attention to the tone of voice they use and the inflection they use on their words. If I say, "Yeah, I hope you have a good day," it could mean anything, depending on my tone of voice, whether I'm nice or super passive-aggressive.

Be open-minded and non-judgmental.

Alan Watts famously says in many of his talks that no human being knows anything, and he's right. At the end of the day, none of us know what's going on in the universe, and there's never a right or wrong answer when it comes to the events of someone's life. We are not in charge of what is going on.

That being said, it's critical to ensure that you're not judgmental when people talk to you, or that you try to be as nonjudgmental as possible, which I know is easier said than done.

However, if you can master this, you will become an excellent listener because you will be focused on what the person is saying rather than your preconceived judgments.

This can be challenging. When someone is talking about something you're passionate about or have strong feelings about, you may already have preconceived notions that the other person is stupid or doesn't know what they're talking about, which means you'll be caught up in your own thoughts rather than listening to the person who's speaking. In other words, you're listening to respond rather than to understand.

Of course, you're free to have opinions and disagree with others, but in many cases, there's a lot of context that you may not be aware of or understand why someone is saying what they're saying. If you can pay attention to this rather than forming your own opinions and making judgments, your listening skills, and thus your relationships with others, will improve dramatically.

A Word About Body Language

There's no denying that body language is important when it comes to listening, and any communication guide you read or listen to will discuss it. Making eye contact with the person you're listening to is a great way to improve how much attention you're paying to them. We appear to be living in a time when this is much more difficult than it appears, and when I was suffering from social anxiety, I literally couldn't do it.

However, with practice, it was a skill I was able to incorporate into my life, and it made my relationships so much stronger. Nodding is a great way to keep someone engaged with you while they're talking to you, and it nonverbally confirms that you want them to continue and that you're interested in what they have to say.

You should also be aware of the speaker's body language.

What exactly are they doing and where are they looking? Are they looking at you, or are they looking somewhere else? Do they appear fidgety and unsure of what they're saying, or do they appear confident and able to hold their own? Body language reveals a lot about us all, and reading it will add a new dimension to your interactions.

And with that, our journey into the world of listening comes to an end. This, like every other aspect and method in this book, is all you need to know. It's simply a matter of sticking with it and putting it into action. Begin small and gradually implement some of these suggestions, and you'll notice significant improvements in your life.

In case you were wondering, no, being in a relationship does not entail simply sitting and listening to what someone has to say in silence. You'll have plenty of opportunities to speak as well, which is what we'll look into now!

Method 5
Improving Conversion Flow

"Nothing beats a good conversation." – Mr. Rich Eisen

We've talked a lot about how to introduce yourself to someone and how to start a conversation in previous chapters. The previous chapter discussed how to give someone your full attention by listening to what they say. However, one critical piece of the puzzle is missing.

What exactly do you talk about?

It's one thing to have the courage to speak up and shake hands with another person, but if you can't carry the conversation forward and end up stalling, sitting in awkward silences, and being generally distant, neither you nor the person you're speaking to will have a pleasant or memorable conversation, at least not in a positive way. If they remember you for being awkward, or even boring, you're unlikely to come across as charismatic, and they're unlikely to want to be your friend. Those are some harsh realities.

To begin with, this isn't something you should be concerned about. There were at least a dozen times when I would fall into this situation while on my self-improvement journey, at least in the beginning. I remember trying to talk to girls (I know, that old chestnut, don't judge me!) and being so confident and charismatic at first.

We got along great and laughed and chatted about something going on across the street, but then something changed and neither of us knew what to say or how to continue the conversation. We basically ended up saying our final awkward goodbyes and never seeing each other again. There's no denying I felt foolish at first, but hey, I'm still alive, and that was years ago. If it happens to you, you might feel embarrassed for the rest of the day, but you'll get over it, and life will go on.

When you can, try to remember this. Because practice makes perfect, the more you put yourself in these situations, the tougher you'll become to them going wrong, but most importantly, the better you'll be at holding your own in a conversation with anyone. This is what I'll be concentrating on in this chapter.

We'll be discussing the art of conversational flow, which refers to the grace and lucidity with which you can navigate different topics, how effortlessly and confidently you can keep talking, and how to have conversations that leave you with a smile on your face thinking, Wow, that was a really good conversation!

We've already discussed the significance of listening, but don't forget that it's a huge part of having a conversation. These are some of the other considerations you should bear in mind.

Be open and honest.

First and foremost, Always be open and honest in your conversations.

We all have a bit of ego that wants to be validated, and we may feel the need to emphasize certain facts about our lives or make something sound much better than it actually was to make ourselves appear better, lucky, or whatever to the person we're speaking to.

This never works. When someone is talking to you and starts boasting or exaggerating, I think you'll agree that it's pretty obvious. You may not notice it at the time, but you will have the impression that something is wrong or that the person is putting on airs.

Validating your ego in front of others is not the best way to connect and make friends. In fact, some people would probably agree it's the worst, so avoid it at all costs.

The science behind this has been written about in Dan Ariely's book The (Honest) Truth About Dishonesty. He writes about how humans can believe themselves to be honest while telling little lies or dishonest truths. Consider yourself and who you are right now. You probably consider yourself to be an honest person, despite the fact that you almost certainly lie about minor details in your life.

However, because you will primarily tell lies about minor matters that you believe are unimportant, you will regard yourself as an honest person. Don't worry, I'm not calling you a liar because this is how most people live their lives. If you're not feeling well but don't want to talk about it, you might say everything is fine when it isn't. You may say you don't know something when you actually do, or you may lie about something you do know when you're not sure.

So, why do we do it?

No matter how you look at it, we're all telling lies, no matter how small, for one reason: to protect ourselves.

You protect yourself from embarrassment, to protect your interests and get what you want, to protect your self-image and how others perceive you, to protect your assets and the things you have, including your energy levels and the time you don't want to waste doing something else, or to protect the emotions and feelings of others.

Lying is simply a method of manipulating reality in order to protect your perception of what is "good and right" in the world. You have an image of what you believe to be the correct way to do things, so you lie to maintain that reality. Isn't it interesting when you look at it that way?

Assume you're at the gym and people are discussing the divisive subject of politics. While you are firmly on the blue side, it appears that everyone else in the room is on the red side. What do you do? Do you lie and say you support the red side to fit in and avoid being judged? Or do you say you support the blue side because it is who you are?

What about lying and not telling the truth to protect the feelings of others, perhaps because you're afraid of hurting their feelings or making them dislike you because they don't agree with what you have to say?

Po Bronson and Ashley Merryman write in their book Nutureshock about how parents will lie to their children about the most insignificant things, and how children will lie to their parents far more frequently than their parents realize. This is because children believe they are telling their parents what they want to hear, which will make them happy, regardless of whether you have stolen some extra chocolate biscuits from the cupboard.

This continues throughout many stages of your life, all stemming from when we were children. Children believe that their parents have huge, unfulfillable expectations of them and that if they don't meet them, it will make them sad, so they lie about what's going on. The study also discovered that when parents confront their younger children about lying, it only convinces them to try harder to lie in the future.

If you want to make friends, you need to work on being yourself, which means stopping all the little lies and just being honest. This entails standing up for what you believe in and remaining true to yourself and your beliefs. If you can do this, you'll eventually connect with people who share your beliefs, and this is where true relationships are formed.

Speak for a Longer Period of Time Than Is Usual

How long do your answers last when you're talking? When I first started talking to people, I used to think that when someone asked me a question, they didn't care about what I had to say and were more interested in themselves. I had the impression that most of the time, people were simply asking because it was the polite thing to do, but if you think that way, are you going to want friendships with them? Most likely not.

When answering questions from others, and this ties into the previous point about just being yourself, answer the question in detail, giving the other person time to relate and keeping the flow of conversation going. Saying your favorite movie is The Matrix, for example, does not invite further discussion. In many cases, people will assume you're just being blunt.

"Hey man, what's your favorite sport?" asks the guy at the gym with whom you're making small talk in the locker room. "Treadmill," you say. Excellent conversation. Everyone wants to be a part of it. Instead, try this: "Hey man, what's your favorite sport?"

"I'm currently running on the treadmill, which is surprising because I used to despise running." I used to love it as a kid, but I haven't done it in ages, and for some reason I really enjoy it now. Is that strange?"

See how much more personality this approach has, as opposed to just giving blunt, unfollowable answers? You're showing so much more of yourself, being so much more confident, and bringing so much to the table. The person you're speaking with also has a plethora of additional conversational topics to draw from. Will they come to an agreement?

Say they both liked and despised it? Is it something they despise? Do they understand your newfound enthusiasm for it? And so on.

According to the Art of Charm website, when talking to someone, always aim for two-sentence answers as a rule of thumb, and one of the best tips to remember is to answer the question directly and then add the "why" to your answer. It's a simple way to start a proper conversation and give the other person something to respond to.

This is a fantastic tip to remember because not only will you have a charismatic, confident conversation, but you'll also learn a lot about yourself and why you think the way you do, giving you even more confidence in yourself!

Choosing the Correct Questions

The final point to consider when it comes to keeping the flow of conversation, well, flowing, is to make sure that you're not just talking about yourself the entire time but that you're asking questions to delve deeper into the other person's life and showing a genuine interest in what they have to say and who they are as an individual.

When I first started going to the gym, there was a guy who was always in the swimming pool at the same time as me.

He used to swim professionally many years ago when he was younger, and all he ever did was talk about himself. I didn't mind because I didn't like talking about myself at the time, but he was so boring. He'd go on and on about swimming and the best way to do the breaststroke and how to train and what to eat and what he did for his job and his wife and kids and how politics is crazy and so on. It was so boring because he never once asked me or my life a question. To be honest, I don't think he knew anything about me during the few months we spoke.

I'm sure you don't need me to tell you that people like this exist everywhere, and the chances are you know someone who fits this description. What are your thoughts on that person? They aren't bad people, but there is no connection or friendship between them. It's just you and whoever else is sitting there listening to this other person talk. If you don't want to be that person, you must begin asking questions.

I titled this section "Asking the Right Questions," and I hope that got you thinking about what kinds of questions you could be asking. The truth is that there are no right or wrong questions, but when it comes to making friends and connecting with others, there is one type of question that outperforms all others: opinion questions.

How do you feel when someone asks for your opinion on a topic that is important to them? It feels fantastic. In the same way that asking someone for a favor shows that you trust that person, asking for someone's opinion works in the same way. "I value your opinion and thoughts, and I want to hear them," you're saying. It is the other person's perception that you are interested in what they have to say that will bring you together.

Try it out for yourself. If you're trying to decide on a movie to watch, a restaurant to visit, a method to approach a project, or which TV show or book to binge next, get someone else's opinion and watch the conversation flow.

As we've discussed throughout this chapter, the best way to keep a conversation going is to focus on the other person and place them at the center of the conversation. You can't go wrong with this method, whether you're asking them questions about themselves, soliciting their opinions, or simply listening to what they have to say.

However, this is not a method that will work for everyone. In fact, no method you could ever learn and try will work with everyone because you simply cannot be friends with everyone. You must seek out people who share your interests and are, in essence, a reflection of yourself.

Method 6
Identifying Your Own Reflection

"Friendship is born when one person says to another, 'What! You too?'" 'I assumed I was the only one.'" - Lewis, C.S.

This is undoubtedly, without a doubt, one of the most important aspects of having a relationship with any human being on the planet. Whether it's with a friend, a partner, a parent, a coworker, or someone else, you must find some kind of common ground here.

There are nearly ten billion people on the planet, which means there is a lot of diversity out there, and not everyone will agree with you.

Consider tribal times, when humans lived off the land, hunting and gathering and trying to survive day in and day out. In these times, we all have a common interest in surviving, whether it's hunting for food or caring for the children, so it's easy to collaborate and work toward a common goal. This progresses as civilization advances.

Some people want to sail boats, while others want to conquer other countries. Some people aspire to be farmers and raise families, while others aspire to be explorers or artists. Some people prefer certain types of music and movies over others in the modern era.

Some people are obsessed with money and fast cars, while others prefer to follow more spiritual paths and practice minimalism, among other things.

What I mean is that we are hardwired to seek out people who share our interests and beliefs. As a result, with each new interaction, your brain searches for a reflection of itself in the people you're speaking with. One study published in the Journal of Social Cognitive and Affective Neuroscience confirmed that common ground is the first thing we look for on a psychological and neurological level when attempting to connect with others.

They used a group of people in their studies and gave them small electrical shocks. Some of the people were friends, while others were strangers, and their brain activity was monitored the entire time. It turns out that when someone else is shocked, the brain reacts differently depending on who that person is.

The brain barely reacts if the person being shocked is a stranger.

However, if the person being shocked is a friend, the brain reacts in the same way it would if you were shocked. "The correlation between self and friend was remarkably similar," said Coan, one of the project's leaders. The findings demonstrate the brain's remarkable ability to model self to others; that people close to us become a part of us, and this isn't just a metaphor or poetry. It's a very real, physical change that takes place."

This means that you are, or will be, a part of the people with whom you surround yourself. According to Gary Vaynerchuck, "you are the average of the five people you surround yourself with," and having common ground with all of these people is how you develop a friend group. Of course, you won't have the same interests as everyone in your friend group, but having some will provide the foundation you need.

It's all about finding this common ground from which to build a relationship when it comes to making new friends and connecting with new people. Returning to my example of the guy who wouldn't stop talking about himself while swimming, he clearly had a strong interest in either swimming or himself. I'm not sure, but my interest stemmed from the fact that I enjoyed being in the water after working out.

There is some common ground here, but not enough to form a connection.

On the other hand, I'm sure we would have gotten along fine if we both loved the idea of competitive swimming. Consider the people you've known throughout your life. You've always had something in common in your relationships, whether it's a shared love of partying, reading, or listening to the same music. It all comes down to finding that common ground.

Time for Action – How to Find Common Ground

So, how do you discover these common interests without interviewing the people you're speaking with and making your interaction feel like an interrogation? Nobody enjoys being questioned. You have a few options, and which one you choose will be determined by the circumstances. Please allow me to explain.

We discussed the first method in the previous chapter, but asking questions is the best way to find common ground. However, it may appear unnatural if you ask forward, abrupt questions, so try to tone it down and make things feel as natural as possible.

For example, asking someone what their ideal vacation would be is a great way to determine their personality. Do they want to stay in a hotel in the mountains and go hiking, or do they want to go to an Ibiza beach party? Sure, you're playing off stereotypes here, but if they fit the stereotype, you'll be able to tell what kind of person they are and whether you have common ground.

What people say reflects back to them, so make an effort to be as present as possible when listening to what they have to say, their body language, and the way they speak. If you're discussing a topic and something like politics comes up, and the person quickly dismisses it and changes the subject, this is an obvious sign that they either don't care about politics or don't want to talk about it.

If, on the other hand, you start talking about fishing, you might notice the other person's eyes light up, and they'll begin talking about all these different aspects of fishing with genuine excitement. If this occurs, you know you've discovered something the other person is interested in.

We've already discussed making your conversations about the other person, and the same is true here. You don't want to start the conversation by saying you caught the biggest fish ever and everyone loved you, and it was amazing because you're just making it about yourself. You must elicit information from the other person.

That doesn't mean you can't talk about yourself, but it does mean you should start with the other person. So, putting all of this together here's the approach you'll want to take. First, listen to what the other person is saying to get a sense of their interests. Continue chatting until you find a topic that both of you are interested in, and then dive in, asking them questions to learn more. Include your own stories and experiences, but not in a boastful manner, but in a way that advances the conversation.

This method is the most effective way to find common ground, and once established, you should notice a new friendship or relationship blossoming right before your eyes.

While this is an effective technique for establishing and nurturing relationships, you've probably heard the adage that you can't please everyone, nor can you be friends with everyone you meet. If you tried, you'd end up faking and lying about who you are in order to fit in, which is not what we're aiming for here.

As you go about your life, building your confidence and interacting with more and more people, you'll meet people you don't like and people who don't like you.

There's nothing wrong with this because you can't be everyone's cup of tea, to use a British expression.

This means you'll need to know how to choose your friends, who you'll spend your energy on, and who you'll engage with for a short period of time before deciding if you actually want a relationship with them, which is what we'll be focusing on in the next chapter!

Method 7
Selecting the Best Friends

"Choose your friends wisely, young people." "Show me your friends, and I'll tell you who you are," an old adage goes. – Not known

It is never easy to choose the right friends. I ended up hanging out with some kids who used to smoke drugs on the weekends, stolen from one of the boys' older brothers, while I was in school. I only tried it once, but I'm not sure why I chose to hang out with them. We had nothing in common, and we didn't like each other very much, and the only time I tried it, we got a warning from the police, which meant I was in a lot of trouble when I got home.

Not everyone out there will or should be your friend. As a person who wants to build strong relationships with others, you must be selective about who you choose to build these relationships with. You want to befriend people who are good for you and will encourage you to be the best version of yourself, especially since you will hopefully want to do the same for them.

Consider some of the people who are currently or have previously been in your life. We've all had toxic friends; you know, the ones who gossip behind everyone's back and say hurtful things, or even bully other friends because they think it's funny even when no one else is. Sure, everyone goes through stages, and some people will pretend to be someone they are not in order to fit in, but as you get older, you should start to see people for who they are.

When you think about it, it's strange. Back in 2015, I worked with a salesman who used to gossip behind everyone's back. We'd have a meeting, and someone would be nervous about giving their presentation, and he'd moan and berate them for being nervous and lacking confidence, as he believed "all men should be." He did this to everyone and about everything, and it never occurred to me that he would do the same to me.

I thought we were friends because he used to "open up" to me with all these little statements about everyone else, but then I overheard him talking about me and how annoying I am with the people he was just berating minutes before, and I realized what kind of person he was. As a result, she was not the type of person I wanted to waste my time and energy on.

The Science of Making Friends

I have a favorite saying, and while it can be phrased in a variety of ways, it basically boils down to this one statement. Read it again and again:

You are the people you associate with.

Assume you have a group of people around you, and there are a total of six of you. You'll be people who know each other quite well because you'll have a relationship based on things like proximity (meaning you'll see each other a lot, whether you're in school, at a club, or at work) and common interests.

However, just because you share interests does not imply that these people are nice. Look at how these people think and perceive the world, and you'll notice that you "borrow" from all of them. Some may even say you're the average of those five people. If you haven't chosen your friends and instead associate with them because they're physically close to you, they may not be the best people for you, nor are they offering you the best kind of relationship you deserve.

This is such an important consideration to bear in mind because the people in your circle of friends, whether obvious or not, will influence so many aspects of your life.

A 2013 study published in Psychological Science discovered that if you suffer from a lack of discipline or low self esteem, spending time with and interacting with strong-willed and disciplined people is the best way to improve these areas of your life.

Similarly, even if you believe you have complete control, the friends you keep will significantly impact your decisions. According to a 2014 survey published in the Journal of Consumer Research, friends play an important role in making financially sound decisions and avoiding impulse purchases. This, however, also works the other way around.

If you like to give in to temptations and spend money easily, your friends can amplify this because you're more likely to indulge together. Whether you look at it from a financial, health, or social perspective, simply being around certain people can put you in a bad situation that you don't want to be in. This is what it means to be criminal partners.

To cut a long story short, if you hang out with and become friends with people who make bad decisions and put people down, chances are you'll make bad decisions and put people down as well.

If you want to lift others up and make good decisions, you should hang out with people who do all of these things.

According to science.

When looking for friends or a relationship, whether professional or romantic, you must ensure that you choose the right person; this may seem easier said than done unless you know what you're looking for. We'll look at some options for doing just that down below!

Taking Things to a Higher Level

Consider the following: What do you want to be doing in five years? Do you want to advance in your career? Do you want to be more fit and healthy? Do you want to travel, have your own home, or start your own business? Whatever you want to accomplish, the people you surround yourself with will be the ones who get you there and help you make the right decisions.

When entering a new relationship, ask yourself, "Will this person help me be the best version of myself, or will they hold me back?" When I first started writing these books, I had a friend who was also self-employed as a personal trainer. We would get together every Friday, have a few drinks, and then just talk about all of our plans and ideas for new projects. We were both working on different projects at the time, but having the opportunity to be open and excited about what we were doing only pushed us forward, and here we are today.

Previously, when I was hanging out with stoners for a year or two, no one wanted to do anything and was perfectly content to stay in the same place they had always been in, with no aspirations to do anything. That's fine if that's what they wanted, but it wasn't the case for me. It was making me unhappy.

Choose carefully who you want to be and surround yourself with people who can help you get there. Naturally, you'll have the same impact on their life. That's not to say you can't talk to people who aren't your friends. It's all well and good to have acquaintance friends and people with whom you can just relax and maybe have a drink once in a while. Nothing is wrong with that. You should consider who your close friends are and who you will devote time and energy to while allowing them into your inner circle.

Discovering Yourself in Others

Finding out what your friend's goals and aspirations are is a great way to see if you could and should be friends, and it goes hand in hand with the last point and the last chapter (so don't worry, I'm not going on about it too much more!). This is why it is critical to find common ground. If you're both able to aim for the same aspiring goals, you'll be able to lift each other up and have a lot more in common, even if your goals aren't the same.

Choose friends who have big goals that are on the same or higher level as yours. It doesn't even have to be something like starting a business, writing a book, or traveling around the world. If you're just getting out of a slump, for example, you might just want to establish a social life with people you see on a regular basis, or you might want to establish good habits like exercising and taking care of your health.

Choosing friends who share your values will help you achieve your goals, whatever they may be.

Choose Friends Who Are Both Givers and Takers.

A friendship, or any relationship, is all about giving and taking. It's a delicate balancing act. You can't have a relationship in which one person does everything for the other person, whether it's money, time, or emotional support, but receives nothing in return.

That's not to say you should give with the expectation of receiving something in return; however, your relationship will be unbalanced, and you'll be left feeling unsatisfied. You'll eventually be filled with resentment for both yourself and them.

This means you should give what you expect to receive and treat others the way you would like to be treated. This is the first and most important rule of friendship. If you can manage this and reduce the number of people who do not treat you with respect, you will find that the relationships you have are far more rewarding.

It's Time to Take Action – Get the Relationships You Deserve

So far, the action times I've shared have all been about making new friends and gaining the confidence to talk to strangers, but this one will be a little different. This time, I want you to look at the relationships you already have and consider whether they are the ones you want or deserve. Don't worry, I'm not suggesting you say something like, "Oh, my girlfriend is pretty toxic, so I'm out."

You don't have to be so rash with your decisions, but take a moment to consider how you feel about the people you spend time with.

You may discover that you're still friends with people you went to high school or college with, but you've grown apart and no longer have much in common. You simply hang out because it is in your comfort zone to do so. It's fine to have these friends, as I mentioned earlier in the chapter. You're not trying to cut people off and say goodbye, but you're thinking about how much of your time you're giving them.

If you're giving them all of your time and hanging out multiple times per week, but you're unhappy and want to spend your time with people who are more like you, you'll need to cut back and find these new relationships that are more suited to who you are right now in your life.

However, if you discover that you're friends with someone who is extremely toxic, you should begin to distance yourself from them.

Don't be concerned; you're not alone in this. There are many people, including myself, who become friends with people who are toxic, but you don't realize it until you think about it and open your eyes.

The truth is that most "toxic" people aren't toxic for the sake of being toxic; rather, they are hurting and dealing with a lot of emotional pain or baggage, possibly from previous relationships or even from their relationships with their parents.

However, it is up to them to work through these traumas, and it is not an excuse to be a bad person.

This is where the decision-making process enters the picture. Are you going to be friends with these people and support them on their journey, even if it gets worse before it gets better, or are you going to spend less time with them to focus on other relationships? It is entirely up to you to make your decision.

These can appear to be significant decisions to make. If you think about your partner and think, "Actually, this person isn't right for me," it can be a difficult state of mind to accept. Give it some time and let things play out on their own in this situation.

Everything will unfold exactly as it should. Just take some time to think about it, talk to the other person about how you feel in the relationship, and allow yourself to see what is truly going on.

This way, you'll be opening the door to beautiful, balanced, and fulfilling relationships in which you invest your time in the right people who are best suited for you while remaining civil with everyone else!

This brings us to the end of this chapter. This section of the book, as promised, is all about sowing the seeds of beautiful relationships, whether that's becoming more confident in yourself or creating opportunities for these relationships to manifest in the first place. However, I've talked a lot about talking and different ways to approach conversations.

There's one aspect of any relationship that we haven't covered yet, and you might want to buckle up for this one because it's possibly the most important yet.

Method 8
Share Your Experiential Learning. Create Memories.

"Moments, not days, are what we remember." Cesare Pavese

Consider all of your best relationships. Think of one relationship in your life that meant something to you and was the most beautiful relationship you can think of. It could be about anyone or anything at any time in your life. Do you have one? Nice.

Consider the type of relationship you had with that person.

Did you go out for coffee once a week but only saw them once? Did you ever see that person outside of work? Did you just see them now and then and catch up on the phone? No, the answer is most likely no to all of the above. In reality, when you think of the most beautiful relationships, chances are you're thinking of ones in which you shared experiences and made memories together.

Remember the concerts you went to, the parties, the sleepovers, the all-night gaming sessions, the dates, the trips to the zoo, the restaurants, the vacations abroad, and so on? It's all well and good to talk the talk and know how to talk to people, but the experiences you share with each other will provide so much more of a connection.

As someone who wants to make friends and become more charismatic, it is up to you to create opportunities for these kinds of experiences to occur, which means training yourself to be a little more outgoing, confident in asking, and creative with the ways you can do things. Are you ready for this one? Let's get started.

The Art of Creating Memories and, As a Result, Great Relationships

What I like best about this concept is how simple it is to grasp.

The human brain may be infinitely complex, and we may not understand half of how it functions, but how it functions on the surface is extremely simple. Friendships exist when pleasure is taken in the company of other people, according to Psychology Today.

When you do something in your life, your brain actively responds by releasing chemicals that make you feel good or bad about the situation. When your body is hungry, you will experience hunger symptoms. After that, you eat, and your body releases feel-good chemicals like dopamine to reward you for taking action. Because your brain wants you to survive, it makes you feel good for performing necessary tasks. So far, you've stuck with me?

These processes go far beyond simple survival. Humans are social beings who rely on the closeness and community of others. Your mind rewards you for spending time with people in the same way that it rewards you for feeling hungry, because being social is hardwired into the survival part of our brain.

We've come a long way since living in caves and relying on one another for survival. Although it is possible to live and thrive completely alone nowadays, your brain will still make you feel lonely and release chemicals and hormones such as cortisol, the stress chemical, because it wants you to interact with other people and be social. That's just human nature.

To elaborate, if you have a bad experience with someone, such as a bully or someone who beats you up or calls you names, your brain will record these experiences as negative and will do everything it can to keep you away from them. This is why, after a painful breakup, seeing an ex can bring up all those old, sad feelings that can make you feel strange, especially if you aren't over them.

You may have agreed to remain friends, but your brain still feels abandoned or betrayed by your ex and will send signals to the rest of you that make you sad and, as a result, want to avoid them. Of course, as with everything we've discussed so far in this book, and what we'll be focusing on for the rest of this chapter, it also works the other way.

When you have a positive, fulfilling, and rewarding experience with someone, your brain releases a flood of feel-good chemicals that record the experience as positive and the people involved as people you want to spend more time with. It's funny because when you look at humans in this light, it's easy to see that we haven't strayed far from the types of people who used to live in tribes and off the land.

This is why typical activities with friends include going out to eat or ordering takeout and then having a movie night. You could do something more exciting, such as attending a music concert, participating in an assault course, or taking a vacation to a beautiful location. Your mind thrives on new experiences, expanding your comfort zone, and having a stress-free and pleasurable time, and it remembers the people you're doing these things with.

Putting it all together, solid and fulfilling relationships necessitate positive experiences. These can range from going somewhere or doing an activity together to being there for someone during a difficult time. Being the person who transforms negative experiences into positive ones is another great way to build relationships, but you can't count on it. Concentrate on creating positive experiences from the ground up.

Positive experiences, according to science and psychology, will relate to you as being a positive influence in the lives of the people you surround yourself with, and relationships can then grow over time.

Time for Action
Get Out and Have Some Fun!

This is possibly my favorite action scene in the book.

I want you to choose someone you're friends with (it doesn't matter if you're close or coworkers), and you want to get closer to them by doing something together. If you're just getting started, start small. This could be something as simple as inviting someone out for lunch or a cup of coffee one afternoon. If you're more confident or closer to someone, you could plan a day trip to the beach or the zoo. You could also go for a walk in a nearby park.

The essence of this stage of the procedure is that it makes no difference what you're doing. It's more about the fact that you're interacting with the other person. Of course, it's good to get lost in your activity, but take some time afterward to reflect on how you felt towards that person during the activity and how your bond with them has grown stronger.

When they say the proof is in the pudding, this is exactly what you'll need, and having a few experiences like this will give you a huge boost in confidence and show you the power of positive experiences. As a quick reminder, in conjunction with the previous chapters, try to take some time to choose a good activity that will suit both of you and will be something you both enjoy (common interests), or allow them to choose something you know they'll enjoy (putting them first).

Have fun and enjoy yourself, but I can't emphasize enough how important it is to reflect at the end of the day on how you feel about the day and the person you spent it with. This is how you will learn and truly understand the impact it can have.

That brings us to the end of Part Two. Are you having a good time so far? Are you studying a lot? With everything we've covered thus far, you should have everything you need to meet new people, nurture relationships with those around you, and begin building your confidence by knowing what to do in new situations.

While we've covered the fundamentals, as we move into Part Three, we'll delve deeper into the advanced strategies that go into taking existing relationships and making them stronger than ever before.

Part Three
Advanced Relationship
Strengthening Teachings

Before I get into the meat of this chapter, I'd like you to consider the following question: What does a strong relationship mean to you?

To many, it means trusting each other, respecting each other, having fun together, and being there for each other when you need it. You want to feel safe and secure with this person, and you want to understand each other. Perhaps it means motivating one another or being committed to one another. Perhaps it means standing by each other through thick and thin.

Whatever a strong relationship means to you, the truth is that the foundations of a relationship come from within you, not from the relationship and connection you have with someone else. Take a moment to think about that.

Assume you're not at ease, confident, or authentically yourself around yourself. In that case, you can't expect you to be yourself around other people, and a truly meaningful relationship will never form. Consider it this way. A parcel may be delivered while you are out and about in your life, such as at work. When the person walks in, you strike up a conversation with them. You talk about the weather and what's going on around you in a friendly tone, and it's a pleasant interaction.

This is known as "putting on airs," because it makes no difference how you're feeling. You'll act the same whether you're feeling extremely positive, extremely negative, or somewhere in between.

While it's understandable to act this way for someone you'll probably never see again or only see in passing, some of us do it to those closest to us.

Raise your hand if you sometimes feel like you're wearing a metaphorical mask when you're with the people around you, and you don't feel like you're acting like your true self. Perhaps you act posher or politer than you are, or you speak in a particular way about subjects you wouldn't normally discuss because you believe that's what the other person cares about, even if you don't. Perhaps you filter yourself and your usual behavior because it may appear inappropriate.

Sure, there will be times when this is acceptable and necessary, but if you want proper relationships with people, you must be yourself and not hide behind masks or filters.

I know it can be difficult, but it is not impossible to "find yourself" and be true to yourself. When you allow yourself to open up and be yourself, you will notice a significant change in yourself, how you view yourself, and your connection with the people around you.

This is what I'll be concentrating on throughout this section of the book. We'll talk about how to be vulnerable, how to be yourself, the art of giving and taking, and how to master how your words can make such a big difference in other people's lives. Anyway, enough of that—get let's started.

Method 9
How to Be Open and Vulnerable

"When we were kids, we thought that once we grew up, we'd no longer be vulnerable. But maturing entails accepting vulnerability... Being alive means being vulnerable." L'Engle, Madeleine

Brene Brown, a well-known psychology researcher, author, and motivational speaker, discusses how being vulnerable is the most important factor to consider when it comes to being happy and forming positive, meaningful, and fulfilling relationships with others. You may be wondering, what does it mean to be vulnerable. Certainly not.

The majority of people associate vulnerability with being weak or damaged. If I ask you to imagine a "vulnerable animal," you're probably picturing a rescue animal before it's been rescued, or one that's been injured and is being hunted by a predator in a nature documentary. In any case, it's not a place you consciously want to be.

But that isn't entirely correct.

When I, Brene Brown, or anyone else interested in happiness and social well-being talks about vulnerability, we're talking about the art of opening up and being your true self, both with yourself and with others. Here's an illustration.

Assume you're in a relationship with someone and you're having trust issues. Your previous partner cheated on you, and now you have these nagging little thoughts, doubts, and insecurities that surface from time to time. They occupy your thoughts and make you unhappy, but you are afraid to discuss them with your partner for fear of being rejected. Because they might think you're silly, weak, or even stupid for having these thoughts, you keep them to yourself.

Anything that triggers these feelings causes you to put up walls and push down insecurities, always trying not to think about them and never opening up and talking about them with others, especially your partner.

This type of situation never ends well. These insecurities accumulate over time, eventually spilling over the edge. You'll resent your partner because they're constantly triggering you, even if you don't realize it at the time. Your paranoid mindset will cause you to repeatedly check your partner's social media or even read through their text messages to see who they're talking to. We all do strange things like this in our relationships from time to time, but is it a healthy relationship? Obviously not.

In order to have a healthy relationship, you must be vulnerable and open about your insecurities. This entails being open and honest with your partner about how you feel and what you're going through. Sure, they may try to assist or may be at a loss for words, but that isn't the point. The point is that you're putting yourself out there and allowing yourself to be open to the world. You're saying that this is me and what I'm going through, good and bad, and that I shouldn't be ashamed of any of it.

Once you've reached this point—and believe me, it's a journey—you'll find it to be a liberating and refreshing experience. Getting there, on the other hand, is a completely different story, and it can be quite frightening.

I know what you're thinking: "Uh, I don't want to open up about what's wrong with me and what scares me." I don't want to be vulnerable. I just want to push all the bad stuff down, never think about it again, and build all those walls to protect myself. Isn't it true that if I don't think about it, it will go away?

Not at all. If you truly want to progress on your self-improvement journey and discover true happiness, even if it's just with yourself and not in your relationships with other people, this is a process you'll have to go through.

There is no denying that researchers such as Brene Brown have pioneered this research field and compiled all of the science behind it over the last few decades. If you want to learn more, I highly recommend her book Daring Greatly or watching her TED talk, which started it all and is still one of the most-watched TED talks to this day. But for now, I'll share some of the key lessons and takeaways I learned from her speeches and books with you here.

Courage is the first step.

It would be wonderful if you could simply snap your fingers, be vulnerable and open with everyone, and focus on being yourself as naturally as possible, but that would be too easy.

Instead, there are some steps that must be taken.

However, the first thing to consider is that, in Brown's words, "vulnerability" necessitates a certain amount of courage. You must be brave, and there will come a time when you must step outside of your comfort zone and take the leap. You could read every book and listen to every podcast on the subject, but there will always be a time when you open up to someone else and lay yourself bare for all to see.

And this takes guts. You may not feel prepared right now, but that's okay. You can gradually work your way up to that. This is why being vulnerable is not a sign of weakness; in fact, it is one of the strongest and most powerful things you can do. You will be able to be your true and authentic self if you follow this path and go for it.

This will come with time, and you can begin by doing small things to build your courage, as we discussed in previous chapters. I'm also not saying you have to lay everything out in front of one person right away. You wouldn't go on a date and unload your entire life on the first night. That's the best way to turn people off because you're oversharing with someone with whom you have no relationship. It all comes down to increasing your vulnerability and how open you can be with someone as your relationship develops.

The best way to proceed is to take one step at a time. Assume you are depressed because you are self-conscious about your weight. You're conversing with someone you're getting to know, and what they say is triggering you. Instead of suppressing your emotions and refusing to speak about them, you must summon the courage to open up and express your feelings. If you hear someone say, "Oh, weight issues are just nonsense. It's just people trying to justify eating poorly," you might want to share your thoughts on the matter.

You don't have to put someone down or take offense; instead, simply express your point of view. There is a lot going on here. To begin with, whether the person agrees or disagrees, they will respect you for voicing your opinions rather than simply agreeing with what they said. They will then either listen to you or ignore you. If they listen and are open to what you're saying, and say something like, "Oh yeah, I suppose I've never looked at it from this angle before," that says a lot about them, and they could be a good friend.

If, on the other hand, they say something like "Ppftt, what do you know?" and are pretty closed off about it, do you really want to be in a relationship with that person? Most likely not.

In any case, it all starts with having the courage to open up and be yourself without apology.

Begin to Discover Your True Self

I've talked a lot about being your "true" or authentic self, and you may be wondering who that is, which is an important part of becoming vulnerable. But how can you be your authentic self if you don't know who you are?

For much of my life, I struggled with social anxiety, and as the years passed, I began to believe that this was who I was. I was the guy who worked in sales and went to work, then went home, maybe forced myself to see a friend every now and then but couldn't wait to get home and just be alone. I was a background guy, single, and barely scraping by. In my journal, I used to write things like "I'm surviving, not thriving."

As I continued to act in this manner, I began to believe that this was my identity. Is there anything I can do to overcome my social anxiety? It's simply who I am at my core. It wasn't the case. Sure, you might be thinking as you read this, "Yeah, I'm a shy, introverted person who gets exhausted speaking to a lot of people." That's all right. What I mean is that we all have these ideas in our heads about who we are, and the more we hear them, the more we start to believe them. What we forget is that we are so much more than the identities we give ourselves.

Self-awareness is one of the most important aspects of becoming vulnerable. This entails comprehending your self-beliefs, how you identify with yourself, and, as a result, who you are. I could write a whole book in itself about this topic, so I'll leave \syou with the main takeaway.

Action Time – Become Vulnerable with Yourself

Start paying attention to your thoughts and emotions.

When anything happens in your life, whether you're watching the news, a movie, or chatting with someone, pay attention to how you feel and what emotions are coming up. When you get a moment, explore those emotions, discover how you feel, and then question why you feel this way. The answers you get may surprise you.

I remember I started doing this by beginning my own meditation practice and keeping a journal. I understand this is not for everyone, so figure out what works for you. Either way, I listened to my thoughts and feelings and realized that I wasn't a shy person who loved being alone. I was just lonely and justifying this loneliness.

Understanding this opened the door for my self-care journey and gave me great insight into where I was in my life and who I am.

When you piece together all these points, you'll start learning about who you are, and you'll start being able to be yourself around other people. Yes, it takes a tremendous amount of courage to open up, but once you do, you'll be opening the door to some amazing relationships that you wouldn't even believe could exist.

Method 10
Opening Your Door to the World

"Your real self may be hiding somewhere, look for it within, when you find yourself, you can freely be what you want to be." – Michael Bassey Johnson

Hand in hand with the last chapter, it's all well and good taking time to learn about yourself and who you are on the inside, but do you know who you are on the outside? One of the biggest problems for me while overcoming my social anxiety was that I had locked myself away in my apartment doing the bare minimum for so many years, it got to a point where I didn't know who I was.

What music and movies did I like? What food did I like? What kind of places did I want to travel to, and what types of books did I want to read? What activities, or exercises, or sports did I like doing? I indeed didn't have answers for these, and if asked, I would just go off the answers I would have given if I was still a teenager. Then, when I think about it, would those answers be the same? No, probably not.

As we change, our choices, tastes, likes, and dislikes change, and if you're looking to get to know someone and have a relationship with them, which is based on the foundations of common ground, then you need to know what you're interested in. This may sound like fundamental stuff, but I want you to take a moment to think about it.

Remember the music you used to like and how that's changed since you were a kid. And movies. Think about your guilty pleasures. All of these things become who you are, and they're not static things. You may hate musicals, and the very idea of them makes you cringe.

Then, one day, you take the time to see one, perhaps not out of choice, and you enjoy yourself. Throughout an evening, something you had no interest in doesn't seem too bad. Your true self is continuously changing and evolving as you go through your life, but only if you let it.

I'm sure everyone would agree that it's easy to get stuck in your ways, especially as you get older and more experienced. Unlessyou're able to open your door to the world and embrace new experiences, even if you're giving them a try to see whether they're for you or not, this is how you grow as a person and understand yourself better. And of course, the better you understand yourself, the better your relationships will be because you won't be settling!

See how it's all tying together?

It's true; there are going to be experiences out there that you don't like. That new sushi restaurant down the road? Yuck. I can't think of eating anything worse than raw fish, but then one day, you give it a go with a new friend, and lo and behold, you don't think it's too bad.

You even agree that you might consider going again. How about that?

Not only are you trying new experiences (which is a chance to connect with people in your life), but you're diving in and seeing whoyou are as a person, giving new things a go, and then making up your mind. What's more, science says that trying new things can be incredible for your brain and mindset.

Dr. Papp of Harvard University wrote: "Until the mid-1990s, we thought that people were born with howevermany brain cells they would die with. We now know that the growth of new cells—a process called neurogenesis—occurs throughout life, even in older age,"

This means your brain is always growing new cells and is changing all the time. If you don't do new things and have new experiences, your brain doesn't tend to grow much because it's familiar with everything around it. Of course, not every day can be a new and wondrous adventure where you try new things, but you don't need to. Doing new things when you can is great for providing yourself with these benefits.

By stimulating your brain in different ways by doing new things and trying new activities, you're allowing your brain to grow in new and exciting ways. This will make you want to do more new things, and this is what it means to be outgoing. Remember how outgoing you were as a kid? It's entirely possible to get that back if you open your mind and say yes to new opportunities.

Action Time – Do Something New!

I bet you saw this one coming.

When I say do something new, you don't need to go for the most outlandish and crazy thing you can think of. I'm not saying go skydiving or take up wakeboarding, but if an opportunity presents itself, such as going to a new restaurant or seeing a play, joining a book club, or taking dance lessons, then this action time is to say yes.

Go into the activity with an open mind and give it your best shot. If you don't enjoy yourself, then that's fine. You're not going to enjoy everything, and you've still taken another step on your journey whenit comes to understanding yourself. However, if you try something new and absolutely love it, you've opened a brand new door, of which there are plenty of beautiful new experiences for you to try.

Don't deny yourself of what could be something amazing!

You can try these new experiences with other people to improve your relationships, or you can take your experiences, and you'll have far more to talk about with everybody in your life. It all starts with you opening your mind to what could be.

Now that the last two chapters have included a bit of time working on yourself and your mindset, we're going to take a little trip back into the art of relationships themselves, this time taking a look at the art of giving and taking, or in this case, not taking.

Method 11
Unconditionally Giving and
Not Taking

"Blessed are those who can give without forgetting and take without forgetting." – Unknown

Method 3 was all about asking for favors and getting people to help you out as a way to spark a connection and build trust, but giving is one of the most fantastic ways to form and build on a friendship. And by giving, I mean truly giving, not just giving because you expect something in return at a later date. In fact, I'm not even referring to the act of giving someone a gift or a physical item; rather, I'm referring to the art of reciprocating.

Peter DeSciolo and Robert Kurzban conducted a study titled "The Alliance Hypothesis of Human Friendship" in 2009.

The researchers discovered that if you want to have a "true friendship" with someone, the age-old adage "I'll scratch your back and you scratch mine" may not cut it. You must go further than this.

When you think about it, the act of helping someone else and having them help you—aka, having each other's backs—makes sense. We've talked a lot about the survival aspect of human nature, and how, as social creatures, we're hardwired to band together to protect one another. For many people, this is the foundation, or at least a key component, of most relationships.

To take your relationship to the next level, you must learn to give without taking, which means to give without expecting anything in return.

I know what you're thinking because I had the same thought.

People will naturally like you if you give and give and give in relationships. You could always pay for coffee, be a shoulder to cry on, organize everything, and always be the one carrying the conversations, but if you never get anything back, this is just someone taking advantage of you, and that's true.

Relationships are a delicate balance of giving and taking, and a line can be crossed. Don't worry; if you believe this is the case in any of your relationships, you will have a strong gut feeling that it is.

It will be difficult to overlook.

The trick is to give in your relationships without losing sight of who you are and without sacrificing your needs, as stated on the Tiny Buddha website. To do this properly, you must strike a balance between being yourself and managing your own life, and then creating a life with someone else. Of course, I'm not only referring to romantic and dating partners. This can be seen in all types of relationships.

What I Mean by "Give"

I'm writing this brief section to ensure that we're all on the same page. When I say you're giving without taking, I mean anything. You may arrive home from work early and decide to deep clean the entire house before your partner arrives. You might order takeout that night if someone in your life has had a stressful day. You may rub their feet in the evening or make them breakfast in bed on the spur of the moment.

You could assist them by purchasing something for them if they are short on funds, or you could simply take them out because you care about them. If they're going through a difficult time, you could have them stay over, or you could stay over at their house, you could do an activity to distract them, or you could sit and talk about their situation with them.

It makes no difference what you give; the point is that you do it because you want to make the other person happy, not because you want something in return. In college, I had a friend who moved in with his girlfriend during his final year, and while he was a normal guy, he had some unusual ways of being in a relationship.

I remember him cleaning up the entire apartment, making dinner, and setting up the lounge all nice for a movie night so his girlfriend could have a night off and relax. On the surface, this appears to be a nice, selfless thing to do, and it's easy to see how doing things like this strengthens relationships by the minute.

However, the two got into an argument, and the night was ruined. When my friend told me about it the next day, he explained that they went to bed after seeing the movie because he wanted to be intimate with his girlfriend. She stated that she was tired and wanted to sleep, but she was grateful for the evening. He became irritated because he felt he had put in so much effort and that his girlfriend was not reciprocating.

He considered her to be self-centered.

Now, I agree with you if you believe this is a very toxic way of looking at things, but there is no doubt that this is a trap that we all fall into from time to time. Just because we do something nice for someone does not imply that they must reciprocate.

It is unconditional when you give without being asked. If the guy I went to college with had realized this, he would have gone to bed with his girlfriend after a lovely evening, and the argument would not have occurred.

Let us fast forward to the future. If he was going through a difficult time, she might consider doing something nice for him. Even if she doesn't, the relationship is still strong because you know that if you're in a bad, stressful situation, your friend, partner, or whoever it is will be there to make you feel better.

In this case, his outburst because he didn't receive anything in return taints the act of giving. Whatever he does in the future, his girlfriend will think, "Oh well, he's only being nice because he wants something in return later," and this way of thinking will contribute to the breakdown of relationships. Instead of simply enjoying each other's company, the relationship becomes about power dynamics, with people calculating who owes who what.

The Value of Boundaries

I've already mentioned that there's a fine line between giving to build a relationship and making someone happy and being used, but you'll have to figure that out for yourself. Assume the man is a decent individual who enjoys doing things to make his girlfriend happy. He plans dates, cooks dinners, and arranges romantic evenings for months, if not years.

However, when nothing is expected in return, the relationship feels empty.

She is constantly out with her friends, and they spend very little time together outside of the events he organizes. They don't connect and don't do activities together, and the relationship feels very one-sided.

This could be a hazardous area. In some cases, the guy may go out of his way to be nice in order to make his girlfriend notice and appreciate him more, but then we're back to square one, with him doing these things because he wants something in return. In this case, he desires her love and affection.

Unfortunately, there are no hard and fast rules about what you should do here, and it is up to you to decide where you draw the line. This is why knowing and understanding yourself is critical.

A healthy relationship is comparable to a dance. You both take a step to the left and a step to the right. Sometimes one of you will take the lead, and then you will switch.

You take turns spinning it. Sure, there will be times when you step on each other's toes and need to re-establish your footing and rhythm, and that's fine. However, if you're constantly trying to catch up or feel like you're carrying all of the weight, this isn't a healthy relationship.

Again, where you draw the line is entirely up to you. If you feel like you're giving a lot but your relationships are very one-sided, talk to the person involved about how you're feeling. Talk to yourself about how you're feeling and why you're feeling that way.

When it comes to giving and taking, this can become a very complicated subject. If you're giving because you want something in return, whether it's a physical or emotional "thing," it could be a sign that you're lonely or invalidated, and you're looking for validation from others. This could be a form of attachment or a manifestation of insecurity, which you should work through by reading or seeking counseling. This has an impact on both professional and personal relationships. Find a happy medium between giving because you care about the person and giving because you expect something in return.

Your relationships will begin to flourish if you are able to find the balance that works for you and have discovered your own boundaries. This is because you will be attending to your own needs for security and validation within yourself, and everything you give to the people in your life will come from a place of love.

It's Time to Take Action – Learn to Validate Yourself

People today give a lot because they want something in return. When I was a kid, I would tidy the house and put all my toys away before my parents got home from work, not because I wanted to live in a tidy house and enjoy having space, but because I wanted my parents to tell me I was doing a good job. This is clearly not a healthy way of thinking because it leads to unhealthy giving.

I want you to think about things you do in your life for other people and then ask yourself why you do them for them during this action time.

Sure, some things in life are unavoidable, such as washing the dishes or sweeping the floors, but pay attention to your thoughts as you do them. Are you buying coffee for your partner because you want them to forgive you for a mistaken comment, or because you simply want to have a pleasant experience with them? Are you putting in extra effort on your work project because you want to do well or because you want to please your boss?

During my time in sales, I spent a lot of time trying to please my boss, which made me resent what I did. Sure, the goal is to make the customer happy and get good results, but I wasn't working to my standards (or boundaries), but I was looking for validation from my boss.

When I changed my mindset to working as hard as I could to complete a project to the best of my ability, and I looked at it and thought, Yes, this is exactly what I'm aiming for, success came to me in ways I could never have predicted. Begin doing things for yourself and validating yourself as you progress through life. Tell yourself you did a good job, and treat yourself with the same kindness you would expect from others.

From here, you'll find your boundaries naturally. You'll be able to give unconditionally to those around you, especially those you care about, which will strengthen your bond beyond belief. It takes practice, but it's a skill that will change your life.

Method 12
Words: The Light and Dark Magical Powers

"Speak with honesty. Only say what you mean. Use the word sparingly when speaking against yourself or gossiping about others. "Utilize your word's power in the service of truth and love." – D. M. Ruiz.

The Four Agreements by Don Miguel Quiz is one of the best books I've ever read. The book describes four Toltec beliefs about how we live our lives and how our minds function. Understanding these beliefs allows us to choose how we want to present ourselves in the world and the type of person we want to be and remove any self-limiting beliefs we may have.

Don refers to the words we use as light and dark magic in one of the most powerful chapters in this book. Don writes beautifully, so I'll paraphrase an example from the book about how the way we talk to people affects not only those people personally but also our relationships with them.

You can pick someone up and place them on top of a mountain using only words, or you can crush them. It is entirely up to you.

The Singing Girl's Story

In the chapter "The First Agreement," who is a fairly normal, intelligent, and kindhearted woman, and her daughter, whom she adored. The mother comes home from work one day, and she's in a bad mood because she had a stressful day at work through no fault of her own.

Her daughter, who is probably five or six years old, is singing when she gets home. Her daughter enjoys singing because it makes her feel free and beautiful. It is her favorite activity. Her mother arrives home, exhausted from the day and suffering from a severe headache, and asks, "Can you please shut up?" "Your voice is messing with my head," or words to that effect.

Now, the mother had no intention of being so aggressive. She was simply acting out in the moment because she was in pain, and the daughter had no intention of antagonizing the mother; she had no idea the mother was in pain. However, the mother's words cut into the daughter, and she began to believe that her voice was horrible and that she was "doing her mother's head in." She believed her mother's words and never sang again, depriving herself of all those lovely, beautiful feelings and depriving the world of the lovely gift she possessed.

Your words have weight. Your words have an impact on your relationships with others, and by understanding the power of your words, you can choose how you want to affect them. Will you use your words (magic) to cast spells of light or to cast spells of darkness on others, as Don so eloquently puts it? It should go without saying that if you use your words to create light, your relationships will thrive.

Words and the Mind's Psychology

There has been so much research into how words affect the brain that it could easily fill several books, so I'll give you the lowdown.

First, how you use your words influences how they are received.

Obviously. The tone, pitch, and intonation of your voice can indicate whether you're happy, sad, passive-aggressive, sarcastic, or something else. It all comes down to how you present what you're saying. One study that looked at the impact of understandable speech on the left temporal lobe discovered that the way we speak affects everyone on an extremely deep, emotional level.

If an ordinary person said, "I have a dream," and compared it to how Martin Luther King said those famous four words, you would have a very different emotional reaction because of how he said it and the emotion in his voice was sending such a powerful message through the words.

Furthermore, other researchers discovered that the language you use reflects how you see yourself and others around you. According to Dr. James Pennebaker of the University of Texas, "the way people refer to themselves and others is highly diagnostic of their mental state."

This means that the language you use paints a picture of you and your situation. If you use negative or depressive language, it reflects how you feel, just as positive, energetic language does.

When asked how your day has been, you could say one of the following things:

"It's been fantastic, thank you."

"It's been consistent."

"It was fine."

"It was just a day."

"Man, it was amazing!"

Even through writing, you can tell what kind of day it was, even though linguistically, they're all pretty close to each other on the "good day" scale, if such a thing exists.

Putting both of these points together—what you say and how you say it—has a significant impact on how people perceive you and recognize you as an individual. Work on what you say and how you say it if you want to be more charismatic. Work on what you say and how you say it if you want deeper relationships. Let us put it into practice.

Action Time: Using Words to Improve Relationships

I want you to slow down your responses and take a moment to think before you speak in any future conversion. That old chestnut of a proverb. Do this in your interactions with others as well as, more importantly, in your interactions with yourself.

For example, if you go to work and say to a coworker that you "have to" work on that latest project, it gives the impression that you're being forced to do something, that you're complaining, or that you're resisting reality. It's a bit of a rant, and repeating it will not win you any friends.

Instead, you could say, "I'm going to start working on that new project." This conveys excitement in what you're doing, and even though you're only working, it creates an entirely new impression of how you view work and how others perceive you working.

Everyone wants to be as enthusiastic about what they do as you are, so in a way, you will be inspiring them to do so.

The proof is in the pudding, so give it a shot and see what happens.

And that brings us nicely to the end of Part Three, or, if I choose my words carefully, to the beginning of Part Four. Part Four is my favorite section of this book because it delves into the mechanics of what the book is about. Still focusing on you, I'm going to give you some real-world advice on how to be more charismatic, confident, and outgoing.

If you take anything away from this book and plan to use any methods, these are the ones you should concentrate on, but combining them with the other techniques in this book will yield amazing results. So, what are you still waiting for? Let us not linger.

Part 4
It's Time to Get to Work on You

While it would be ideal if life worked like this, you can't just snap your fingers and decide to be more charismatic and confident. From a mental and psychological standpoint, you can, but taking action to become more confident takes time and practice, just like anything else in life.

What I would recommend for this section of the book is to read it through, let the information sink in, and then begin practicing a little at a time. Some aspects will be more appealing to you than others. Some parts you may have already done, while others you may not have considered, so choose the parts you want and work with them. If you're in the mood for something spicy, go ahead and try something you've never tried before.

My point is to experiment and figure out what works best for you. This way, you'll be discovering yourself and your charismatic style along the way. Let's get started!

Method 13
Increasing Your Charismatic Potential

"Charisma is the perfume of the soul." Toba Beta

One of the main goals of this book was to help you understand what it takes to be more charismatic in yourself and in your relationships.

While you are already familiar with many methods, this chapter focuses on the hard and fast things you can do to actively become more charismatic. So, first and foremost, what do I mean by "charisma?"

Being charismatic means having the charm and attractiveness about you, both physically and intellectually, that makes others want to be around you and learn more about you. You may entice people by the way you speak and act, or you may inspire people to be better by what you say and do.

I'm sure you know some charismatic people in your life, the types of people who make you want to be them, but not in an egotistical way—rather, in a natural way that just makes you feel at ease around them. Fortunately, anyone has the potential to be this type of person. It's something you have to learn and practice, though some people are born with it. This is how. By the way, these are all action times in and of themselves!

Understanding Your Values

It's impossible to be self-assured and charismatic if you don't know what you stand for. This means you must be aware of your values as well as your abilities. What do you stand for, what do you believe in, and how much potential do you have to make an impact in your life?

The answer to the last question is an enormous amount.

You can achieve great things if you put your mind to it, but you won't be able to do them unless you truly believe you're capable of doing them. Without this belief, it is impossible to be charismatic because you will believe that your abilities are limited. Of course, you have limitations, but being aware of them is critical because you can be confident while also admitting that there are things you can't do.

Personal Integrity

Integrity is the ability to stick to your values and do what you say you'll do. This is critical when it comes to trusting relationships and those around you, as well as believing in yourself.

For example, if you declare that you are going vegan but continue to eat meat, you are saying that your values do not align with your actions.

As a result, you lose credibility in the eyes of others.

The bottom line of this point is to avoid doing things that are contrary to your values. Of course, your values can change over time, especially as you learn more about the world from others and your experiences, but you don't want to be corrupted by others.

Assume you value keeping your head clear and not smoking because it is unhealthy, but you go to a bar and someone offers you a cigarette, and you succumb to temptation or peer pressure. This indicates a lack of integrity because you aren't standing up for what you believe in, which isn't a very charismatic way to be.

Consider Yourself

You've probably heard the expression "to be a sheep," which means to simply follow everyone else and believe what they say. Because you're not thinking for yourself and making your own decisions, this isn't a very charismatic way to be. The most charismatic people think for themselves, regardless of what the majority believes, which is why they are such inspiring people to be around.

The best way to accomplish this is to not take everything at face value, but rather to dig a little deeper.

I recently spoke with a man who had spent his entire life working in a factory and complained about how health and safety regulations had gotten out of hand. I told him I could see his point, but if he had lost a family member due to poor workplace health and safety standards, he would probably see things differently.

The sheep way of thinking is to agree with everything, perhaps the majority opinion of those around you. A charismatic person, on the other hand, will take the time to consider things from various perspectives before making up their minds and perspectives. Furthermore, a charismatic person can change their mind quickly and is not bound by a single way of thinking. This, in and of itself, is a very appealing trait.

Have a Fire Within You

Nothing is more appealing than having a flame or a spark inside you that drives you to go out and get what you want in the world. It took me a long time to get started writing books when I first decided I wanted to do so. I'd toss and turn, write drafts, and then abandon them for months on end, convinced that I wasn't good enough and that it wouldn't work.

Is this an appealing and inspiring way to live? Clearly not.

After working on my charisma and confidence, this began to light a fire in me, a burning passion for writing, and once I acknowledged that fire within me, I knew there was nothing that could stop me from doing the things I wanted to do. The most charismatic people discover this fire within themselves and will go to any length to maintain it. This is the energy that draws people in.

When it comes to your own life, ask yourself what makes you happy and passionate about it. What aspects of your life make you feel alive? These aren't answers you'll get overnight, and you might already have some ideas, so look for them and pursue them. Nothing is more appealing or charismatic than a person who is ambitious and driven to make the most of life.

Push Yourself Outside of Your Comfort Zone

Charismatic people are unafraid of being uncomfortable.

There will always be times and situations in your life when you feel uncomfortable and uneasy, but how you respond and act in these situations will define you as a person. Do you avoid these situations at all costs, or do you bravely confront them and do everything you can to make the most of them?

It is entirely up to you to make your decision.

Rather than fleeing from uncomfortable situations, putting yourself in them or simply accepting them forces you to expand your comfort zone. Instead of remaining stagnant and where you are, this will help you grow as an individual. This means you'll be more open to new opportunities, becoming more outgoing and naturally charismatic as a result.

I still have social anxiety on occasion, and there are definitely days when I'd rather stay in and watch Netflix. It would be so easy for me to say no to an invitation to go out with a friend and just do nothing. I recognize this mindset, however, and will instead say yes, forcing myself to attend the event.

This is always the right decision for me, and I will buzz off the connection I receive from other people, which means I can become more energetic and confident in myself and have the opportunity to form new relationships. To summarize a long story, push your boundaries and limits, do things you don't want to do, and make the best of any situation.

Take Charge of Your Emotions

Being an emotional person is a bad situation. Now, I'm not saying this because I think emotions are bad. Emotions are useful because they reveal who we are as individuals and what we care about. However, allowing your emotions to consume and control you is where things can go wrong.

It's like when you're driving and someone cuts you off or makes a mistake, and you feel a wave of rage wash over you. You have the option of allowing that emotion to control you and ruin your day, or of letting it go and not allowing it to bother you. This requires you to be aware of your emotions and how you're feeling, and then choose how you want to react rather than reacting and acting based on the emotion itself.

You are not in control of your life if you are a slave to your emotions and allow them to control you. If you feel sad and act and communicate with others through that sadness filter, you're not yourself, and this is where problems arise. If you have an emotional conversation with a partner, such as during an argument, you may say things you don't mean, which can lead to more problems and many regrets.

To be charismatic means to be emotionally stable and in control. Instead of allowing them to use you as a puppet, you are mindful of them and act in accordance with how you feel. This enables you to become much more grounded and rational about everything that happens in your life, which is a commendable trait to have.

If you stick to these points and work on them where you can, you'll notice a significant improvement in your sense of self, as you'll become far more charismatic and confident in yourself. People will also become drawn to you, attracted to you, and want to form relationships with you. You'll also feel far more fulfilled in yourself, which will improve your overall life satisfaction.

While many people use the terms charisma and confidence interchangeably, and they are somewhat similar, I'm going to devote the next chapter entirely to improving your confidence and understanding the key differences between the two.

Method 14
All You Need to Know About Confidence

"It is our faith in our bodies, minds, and spirits that allows us to seek out new adventures." Oprah Winfrey's

As with the previous chapter, and to ensure that we're all on the same page as we progress through this one, the official definition of confidence is having the willingness to act appropriately when confronted with life's challenges and the drive to succeed. This goes hand in hand with getting out of your comfort zone, putting yourself in uncomfortable situations, and even embarking on a journey to become more charismatic while believing in yourself.

If you lack confidence, you will lack the ability to be the best version of yourself. You must have that passion and inner motivation in order to step into your true self and be yourself. This is essential for your relationship with yourself, and it has ramifications for every other relationship you'll have in your life, including the ones we've discussed in previous chapters.

As previously stated, all of the following sections of this chapter are actionable, so there is no need for action here. Simply go over each point, see what resonates with you, and figure out what works for you.

Take note of these tips and guidelines to help you become the most confident version of yourself.

Discover Your Limiting Beliefs

There will be times in your life when you are naturally confident, so a good place to start when trying to expand this confidence "zone" is to consider where you are not so confident. Are you not as outspoken when you're around strangers? Do you withdraw when you're around your parents? Do you ever feel like you're being overshadowed at work? When you're trying to improve something in your life, you need to know where you're starting from, and that's exactly what you're doing here.

Sit down and make a list of times in your life when you feel shy and insecure—just making this list should be enough to highlight what areas of yourself you'll want to work on. Make another, more condensed list of what areas of your life you want to be more confident in, and then get to work!

Establish Your Confidence Style

Everyone is self-assured in their own unique and personal way, and while being loud and outspoken may suit some people, others prefer a quieter, more humble approach. You may fall on either end of the spectrum or somewhere in the middle, so figure it out and you'll know what to aim for.

The best way to do this is to recall times in your life when you were most confident. What were you doing and where were you? What were you doing? When you figure out why you felt so empowered in those moments, you'll be able to apply these concepts to other areas of your life.

Minimize In comparison to Others

"Comparison is the thief of joy," Elon Musk once said, and it's so true it hurts. Everyone is unique and follows their own path in life. Comparing yourself to someone else and their position will only make you feel bad about yourself and diminish your accomplishments. The only person with whom you should be comparing yourself is yourself.

Assume you're about to give a presentation at work, but you're comparing yourself to some of the world's best TED talk speakers. Of course, your presentation will pale in comparison to those of these experienced speakers, but that doesn't mean you're a bad or unworthy candidate. Always strive to do your best and recognize that experience will always help you improve. When you compare yourself to yourself rather than to others, you'll find that you gain confidence in everything you do.

Continue to Learn

If you close your mind to new ways of learning, you will become stagnant, much like a flowing river that stops flowing and becomes a murky pool of water. When you take the time to learn something new, whether it's a new fact about the world or a new skill, you'll give yourself a confidence boost because you're proving to yourself that you're enough and fully capable.

Always be willing to learn new things, and you'll be amazed at what it can do for your mindset and how much it can boost your self-esteem.

Be Honest to Yourself

Yes, we've returned to this point, but I can't help but emphasize how critical it is. Assume you're masking yourself and pretending to be someone you're not for the sake of others. In that case, you won't be confident in yourself because you'll be focusing all of your energy on hiding this person.

There is no reason to spend energy hiding yourself when you can freely be yourself and truly embrace who you are. Consider who you are, then write down who you are and what makes you who you are. This relates to the previous chapter, where we discussed understanding yourself and your values and having the integrity to stick to them.

When you are true to yourself and reflect this to those around you, you will be able to be your genuine, confident self, with nothing to hide from anyone. Because people know who you are and can relate to you, this naturally opens up new opportunities for relationships.

That brings us to the end of this method. Developing confidence using the methods outlined above will take time and practice, as will the rest of this book, but if you start with a few things, you'll notice significant improvements right away.

Simply take the time to snowball these results and keep the momentum going!

While we're on the subject of self-assurance, I'd like to devote a chapter to discussing outward appearances. We've talked a lot about working on your inner self and discovering who you are so you can share this person with others and form amazing relationships, but what's on the outside also matters. Please allow me to explain.

Method 15
Your Outside Is a Mirror of Your Inside

"Loving oneself is the start of a lifelong romance." Oscar Wilde's

Two things were discovered in a 2019 study published in the International Journal of Environmental Research and Public Health.

One, poor hygiene habits are a major risk factor for preventable diseases. And, secondly, poor hygiene is a risk factor for social rejection. That makes sense.

During my second college year, I worked a summer job in a factory, and there was a guy there. He had to be in his 30s, and his breath was terrible. And I'm not talking about the kind of breath where he may have eaten something that morning and it's stuck in his teeth. I'm referring to persistent bad breath that seemed to get worse by the day. He was a nightmare to work with at the time, but his lack of hygiene only made matters worse.

Consider yourself in this situation. If you're at work or in a bar—or any social situation—and you're talking to someone who has bad body odor, will you focus on what they're saying or will you try to get away from them? Most likely the latter.

Similarly, if you see someone walking down the street wearing filthy clothes and not looking like they care about themselves, do you want to associate yourself with this person? In the opposite direction, do you think people will want to associate with you if you appear to be uncaring about yourself?

Being a good, genuine person is admirable, but if you don't take care of yourself, you'll push people away. More realistically, if you don't take care of yourself, you're unlikely to be confident in yourself, which will lead to you being even more socially anxious than you already are, making it difficult to form and maintain relationships.

To make a long story short, it pays to take care of yourself and treat your body with respect, both for the attraction of others and for increasing your confidence in yourself. Everything else will fall into place naturally if you look and feel the part of the person you want to be. In this chapter, we'll look at some of the things you can do to take care of yourself.

Discover Your Personality

Everyone has their own style, so finding yours is essential for your confidence and self-esteem. What kinds of clothes do you like to wear, and what clothes make you feel the most comfortable? It's a good idea to try on different clothes to see what you like and don't like, and don't just stick with what you've always liked.

During the height of my social anxiety, I would only wear tracksuit bottoms and hoodies in black, and nothing else. However, after reading up on how we should dress to be comfortable, not just for other people, I dug out some old button-up shirts and began wearing them. The benefits were immediate. I felt so much better about myself, and even choosing nice clothes for myself to wear boosted my self-confidence and made me feel as if I was putting effort into myself. This then began to spread to other areas of my life.

Even if you're not into fashion, taking the time to select and wear clothes that make you feel good can have a huge impact on your confidence and self-esteem. If you want to empower yourself, this is one of the best approaches to take.

Create a Daily Routine

Proper hygiene is essential if you want to feel confident in yourself and attract others. I'm sure you've encountered people with poor hygiene who made you want to be somewhere else rather than next to them. Don't be like that!

Creating a daily and weekly routine is the best way to stay on top of your hygiene efforts. Brushing your teeth twice a day for two minutes at a time, thoroughly washing your skin in the morning and at night, and wearing fresh socks and underwear every day should all be part of your daily routine.

You can also create a skincare routine if you want to use products to treat specific conditions, such as dry skin or acne. Other essential hygiene tips, such as flossing, using mouthwash, and shaving or plucking brows, should be done on a regular basis. What you do is entirely up to you. It's simply a matter of putting in the effort to see what you can do and then sticking with it until it becomes a habit.

Even learning how to brush your teeth properly can make a world of difference. I had a bad wisdom tooth experience that made me realize how important dental care is. I purchased an electric toothbrush that connects to an app that tracks where you brush your teeth and how much pressure you apply to the brush. It works perfectly.

All of this adds up to you taking the time to care for yourself, which helps you love yourself more and makes you incredibly appealing to those around you.

Regular exercise is essential.

I know you probably saw this one coming, but it's an important part of taking care of yourself. Exercise regularly will give you so much more energy as you go through your day if you can get it down to a routine where you don't even need to think about it; you'll be fitter, healthier, happier, and more satisfied with your life, and all of this will make you feel good about yourself and attract other people if you're working out and looking your best.

Again, you don't need a strenuous exercise regimen; instead, take the time to figure out what you want to do and how to make exercise enjoyable. Do you enjoy jogging, swimming, or running? Do you want to be a part of a group? Would you rather go to the gym or work out outside? Experiment with all of the options available to you to see which activity you connect with, thereby narrowing down the activities you're more likely to stick with for longer periods of time.

Exercising is important for maintaining a balanced state of mental health, reducing stress, and increasing confidence, according to numerous studies. When you exercise with a partner or a friend, join a team, or improve your ability to successfully create powerful and beneficial habits, you will also improve your social relationships.

Consume a Healthful Diet

Eating a proper, healthy diet goes hand in hand with exercising properly and taking care of yourself in the best way possible, allowing all of the positive benefits to enter your life. Now, this isn't a traditional diet point, and I'm not going to go on and on about how you should cut out a bunch of foods and be strict by making meal plans and punishing yourself if you order takeout.

Sure, you can be strict if that's what works for you, but if you're more of an average person, here are some easy tips.

First, increase your intake of fruits and vegetables. You should aim for five full portions per day, which roughly translates to 80-gram portions. That's equivalent to 80 grams of grapes, an apple, or a large banana. You can eat vegetables any way you want, whether frozen, fresh, dried, or juiced, which is great if you don't want to spend a lot of money on food. You can simply shop in the most convenient manner for you.

Second, try to limit your snacking. Eat three consistent meals per day, avoiding skipping breakfast, and limiting snacking between these meals. You obviously can if you're hungry, but eating three meals per day at set times helps to establish a rhythm and natural pattern in your body, which will benefit digestion and give your body the energy it needs to get through the day.

You could also experiment with intermittent fasting. I would do your own research because there are many options available, but the best option that worked for me was only eating between the hours of 12 p.m. and 8 p.m. This allows the body to digest food for 16 hours and allows you to rest and digest properly.

Additionally, make sure you're not overeating sugar, fatty foods, or salt. The final factor to consider is drinking enough water, with a daily intake of two liters being recommended.

Getting a one-liter bottle was one of the best purchases I ever made because you only need to fill it up twice a day and you'll know when you've had enough. The benefits of this water point alone will bring about a significant improvement in your life.

Now, I could go on and on about all the health tips you could follow, and I could write a whole other book just about that topic, but thankfully, there is a wealth of information available online. Remember, before making any drastic changes to your lifestyle, take things slowly and consult with a healthcare professional, especially if you have a physical condition.

To bring everything full circle, if you can take care of yourself physically, your confidence and self-esteem will skyrocket.

You'll feel better about yourself, which will have a huge impact on your new and old relationships. People will want to spend time with you, and you will want to spend time with them. By following these tips, changes will occur in your life, and you will naturally be able to look back in a few months and be amazed at everything that has occurred.

Are you ready for the final characteristic you must possess in order to form healthy relationships?

Method 16
Trust is Everything

"Trust takes years to build, seconds to break, and eternity to repair."

– Not known

If you've ever been lied to or betrayed by someone, you understand how devastating it is to have trust in a relationship broken. Trust is essential in any relationship. Even if you consider yourself to be a trustworthy person, it is critical that you consider how you can be more trustworthy and demonstrate this to those around you on a consistent and natural basis.

Consider how often you tell yourself little white lies. The lies that have no meaning but are told anyway. In the sales industry, I used to say all the time that I was finished with a project and would send it over on Monday because my internet was acting up. The work was not completed. I was just sitting at home wallowing in self-pity and making up excuses to give myself more time. You may believe that these lies are harmless, but when people see through them, they create an impression of you and harm your relationships.

From the other person's point of view, they notice you're going through a difficult time but don't want to approach you. You're obviously lying because you don't want to talk about it. However, that person will hold a grudge against you because you lied to them, and while it may seem insignificant, they will not trust you on much larger, more important issues.

Consider this scenario: you tell your boss, "I haven't been able to do the work because I've been struggling this week." I'm sure I'll have it finished by Monday. "I just need some time to get back on track." Sure, there's probably a voice in your head telling you that wouldn't go over well, but at least you were honest, and your boss is far more likely to respect you for saying this, which will improve your relationship with them. It's a very respectful thing to do.

According to a 2016 global study of some of the world's top CEOs, 55 percent of CEOs in the world's largest companies said that a "lack of trust" was one of the biggest threats to a company's stability and success. As in my previous example, if you don't trust the people you work with, it causes a significant shift in the team dynamic because no one knows who is telling the truth. Problems are unavoidable at some point.

The same is true for your relationships. If you break trust in a relationship, whether romantic or friendship, the person involved may never fully trust you again, and there is no stability. It makes no difference what you say to that other person; they can simply say, "I don't believe you," and there's nothing you can do to change their mind.

As a general rule, always be truthful with people from the moment you meet them. Give them no reason to suspect you're untrustworthy. Your relationships will be stronger than you can imagine if people can trust you with their lives. So, how do you go about it?

How to Improve Your Relationship Trustworthiness

Of course, I could just say that you shouldn't tell lies at this point, and that would suffice, but it isn't. People have varying life experiences, and if you meet someone who has been lied to by people in their lives for as long as they can remember, they may not trust you, even if you are a trustworthy person. You must have the integrity to demonstrate this, and you can do so by following the steps outlined below.

Begin Slowly and Build Trust

We've already discussed how important it is to be vulnerable, which is brought up again here. You must be vulnerable in order to build trust. If you tell people openly and honestly about how you think and feel, you're telling them that you're an open book and that you can be trusted because you're trusting them with what you're telling them.

However, it's important to remember that when you're getting to know someone, you don't just dive right in and share all of your baggage. As previously discussed, this is referred to as being "too vulnerable." Begin slowly when getting to know someone, gradually progressing to more intimate and vulnerable details of your thinking. Remember that while you want the other person to trust you, you also want to be able to trust them, so strike the right balance of giving and taking.

Putting in the Work

Assume two people are working in the same office. They've been working in the same office for 30 years and only speak in passing.

They discuss the weather and exchange brief statements about company changes. Despite knowing each other for so long, you wouldn't call them close or even friends.

Compare that to two people who collaborate on projects in the same office. They've only been working together for two months, but they're very close, they talk about work every day, they share their social lives, and they have to deal with both the good and the bad at work.

The relationship, despite being in physically similar circumstances, produces two very different relationships. Trust does not happen overnight, nor does it come easily. If you want someone's trust, you must invest time and have interactions with them. The more positive time you invest in the relationship, the more likely it is that you will be trusted.

Avoid Inflicting Emotional Harm on Others

When someone tells you something they trust you with, you must respect them and avoid damaging or hurting them, even if you do so unintentionally. This is one of the quickest ways to lose someone's trust.

Assume someone is telling you something about their private life that they have been hesitant to share with anyone else. Perhaps it's private, or perhaps they believe no one else cares. The worst thing you can do is dismiss that person, make them feel inferior, or treat them with contempt, disgust, or condescension.

The more intimate your relationship with someone is, the more important it is not to cross a line because your words will be more powerful.

Remember that your words have the power to create magic, and the spells you cast are entirely up to you.

This doesn't mean you can't be honest with the people in your life about how you feel, or that you have to effectively shut up and listen.

It means you should be aware of how you're reacting to something. If someone tells you about their partner, keep in mind that you're only hearing one side of the story, and it's an emotionally tainted side at that, so don't judge or jump to conclusions.

In many cases, you don't need to give advice unless someone asks for it, and the person is instead speaking to you to get something off their chest. A great way to deal with this point is to simply respect them and give them the benefit of the doubt until proven otherwise, regardless of the situation. This way, you can keep your connection and trust no matter what happens.

Be Open About Your Feelings

Just as in the example at the beginning of this chapter, you must remain true to yourself and others around you, even when it is difficult and difficult to do so. Telling the truth can be difficult at times because you are afraid of hurting others, disappointing them, or putting yourself in a bad light.

The best relationships, however, are formed between people who can be open and honest, even when it is easier not to. This will earn you a lot of respect from the people in your relationships, and the trust will only strengthen these bonds.

With all of the information in the chapters we've covered in this section of the book, you should have more than enough to work with. When it comes to working on yourself, I want to remind you not to try to change everything all at once, nor should you try to change yourself because you believe you need to.

You are perfectly adequate for the world just as you are, and this is a mantra you should repeat for a significant boost in your self-confidence! However, regardless of how you look at it, everything in life is a skill that can be honed. All of the points we've discussed are scientifically proven to have a positive impact on your life. These will help you to be happier, more fulfilled, and healthier in general, and the effects will be felt throughout your relationships.

Part 5
Maintaining Relationships and Looking Forward

And now we come to Part Five. We've covered everything you'll need to know about increasing your charisma, building your confidence, making friends, attracting people to you, and developing all of your relationships, from your professional connections to your romantic partners, and everyone in between and on either side.

In this final chapter, I'll leave you with three methods to keep in mind for the future of your self-development journey. This is how you spend your time with people, how you develop patience with yourself, others, and your entire life journey, and how you learn to forgive.

Method 17
Time: Priority Is Given to Quality Over Quantity

"Relationships are built on small, consistent time deposits." You can't cram for the most important things. If you want to connect with your children, you must be available on a consistent basis, not on a whim." Andy Stanley's

When I was a teenager, I was involved in some clingy relationships. I had maybe two best friends and would jump from one romantic relationship to the next, spending all of my time with these people. Now, I had a large group of friends, but I rarely saw them. For some inexplicable reason, I assumed that I would spend all of my time with the same people, and that this was how life worked.

It doesn't work like this, and it's a very unhealthy way to live.

You shouldn't spend all of your time with someone just because you love them or have a connection with them. The time you spend with people—anyone, really, not just those close to you—should be quality time. A couple of hours of quality time once a week, or even once in a while, could suffice. Everything is dependent on the individual relationship.

Spending too much time with someone can be detrimental to your relationship because you are not allowing each other to see other people, thereby gaining a fresh perspective on the work, and you do not have alone time to be alone, process emotions, and think your own thoughts free of distraction. Even if we don't want to admit it, we all need time alone now and then.

According to a 1999 study by Zimmer and Gembeck, women who jump into new relationships and spend a lot of time with their partners spend less time with their friends, which causes problems in both the romantic relationship and the friendship.

If you spend all of your time with a small group of people, any goals or aspirations you have will be impossible to achieve because where will you find the time? You'll also be impeding the progress of the people you're spending time with, which can lead to attachment and resentment. If you're resentful of each other, even if you're not aware of it, it will cause problems in your relationship.

So the best thing to do in this situation is to take a step back and find balance.

Along with making memories and having positive experiences with others, don't spend all of your time with people you care about; instead, remember to be an individual and live your own life. Other people in your relationships should not be your entire life, but rather people who complement and contribute to it.

Have Some You Time – It's Action Time!

You'll appreciate this action time because it feels so good and energizing when done correctly. I'd like you to disconnect from the outside world for an hour or so once a week. This entails switching off your phone or, at the very least, blocking your social media apps.

Watch a movie from beginning to end, read a book, learn a language, meditate, take a bath, or do whatever you want, but do it as quality time with yourself.

Give yourself the same amount of attention and love that you would give to someone you care about. You'll be able to connect and stay connected with who you are as a person if you do this on a regular basis, and you'll be able to bring this truly-loved self into your relationships.

Method 18
Developing Journey Patience

"Losing patience means losing the battle." – Mohandas Karamchand Gandhi

You'll need patience to develop yourself, get to know someone, deal with a difficult time in your relationship, or basically deal with any kind of situation in life.

When it comes to relationships, if you don't have patience, you'll find that stressful situations start to snowball.

When something happens, we take it personally, or the other person struggles to find the right words to say, we may become irritable, defensive, or even lash out and say something we don't mean. This will only exacerbate the situation, causing more stress and, as a result, more problems, and the vicious cycle will continue.

Developing patience is all about feeling those initially stressful emotions, taking a deep breath, and then remaining grounded and calm. Let's say someone at work is freaking out because a part of the project hasn't been completed, and the client is putting pressure on the boss. Everyone is getting tense right now.

Instead of freaking out with everyone else and watching the team disintegrate (some people getting thrown under the bus and people starting to point fingers), you remain calm and let everyone have their turn. When it comes to you, you speak calmly, emphasize the work that needs to be done, and then what solutions are available. This will earn you a lot of respect from those around you.

If you go through life with a hurried attitude, you will be the only one who suffers. Always take the time to look at things, even the most difficult situations, from a calm point of view. This can, admittedly, feel impossible to do at times, especially when the people you're interacting with are impatient. Still, staying cool, calm, and collected is always a good idea for your mental health.

Action Time – How to Improve Your Patience

There are numerous ways to improve one's patience. To remind yourself to be more patient throughout the day, you could meditate, journal, or even write affirmations on your hands. I experimented with setting alarms on my phone that were labeled with "be more patient" texts to remind me at random times.

However, the single most important way to become more patient, and the act that worked for me, was to simply breathe. This is probably a form of meditation, but it didn't matter what I was doing or who I was with. I began to practice taking a deep breath before doing or saying anything. I didn't make it too obvious, but it was more of a deliberate breath. This was something I did even when I was in a good mood, such as when I was out with friends.

This inhalation served as a reminder to be patient. When I eventually found myself in a less-than-desirable situation for which I didn't have to wait long, I would breathe and stay patient, which meant I was much more grounded when it came to answering other people and thinking clearly. This process helped me develop a much more positive outlook on life and strengthened my relationships

Method 19
The Ability to Forgive

"There is no love without forgiveness, and there is no forgiveness without love," Bryant H. McGill once said.

I saved this point until the end because I wanted to go out on a high note.

I read about ImmaculeeLlibagiza's story before starting to write this book. Indeed, it was her story that inspired me to write this book in part because it is so powerful and demonstrates how many of us are missing out on such an important aspect of our relationships.

Every person on the planet is and will always be a human being. It may seem obvious, but so many of us forget that being human means we can and will make mistakes throughout our lives. Even if we try not to, we will inadvertently hurt others, and others will inadvertently hurt us.

Learning about the power of forgiveness, on the other hand, can change everything.

I briefly mentioned being cheated on by my ex-girlfriend a few years ago and being so angry that I punched a windscreen; this was hatred and anger I carried for years. I blamed my sadness and pain on my ex, and when I found myself in new relationships, I carried that resentment with me, and it affected me in so many ways. I had trust issues, was paranoid, and simply expected to be hurt again. It wasn't my new partners or friends who were at fault; it was me. I hadn't figured out how to let go of the past.

ImmaculeeLlibagiza's Story

ImmaculeeLlibagiza was born in Uganda and witnessed the genocide and traumatic events that ravaged the country as a young girl. Immaculee was hiding in a Catholic priest's bathroom in his house with a group of other girls as the militia came through to kill anyone who wasn't of the superior religion.

The bathroom was three by four feet in size. While the priest expected to hide the girls for a few days until the militia moved on, the genocide lasted several months. Immaculee remained in that cramped bathroom, surrounded by other girls, for several months, never speaking a word to anyone for fear of being discovered. While the house was being raided multiple times, the bathroom door was hidden behind a bookshelf.

The government was eventually deposed, and a new party was elected.

The perpetrators of the genocide were apprehended, and the country was retaken under control, but not before the rampage killed over a million people. When Immaculee emerged from the bathroom, she realized she had left everyone behind. Her mother, brothers, and close friends. Everyone had been murdered. Her small town had been completely destroyed.

Immaculee had spent her time in the bathroom reading the Bible over and over, praying to God that everything would be okay, and it was here that she learned about forgiveness. Years passed, and she was given the opportunity to visit the man who murdered her family, who was imprisoned.

When she arrived, the guard offered to hold the man so she could hit him, spit on him, and do whatever she wanted to exact revenge on the man for killing all those people, just as other people had done for years when they visited. The man appeared to be broken.

Immaculee, on the other hand, did the unthinkable. She sat across from him, took his hand in hers, and said, "I forgive you." That was such a powerful moment.

The Ability to Forgive

Many of us will never be in a situation like Immaculee's, and reading her story may make you consider how much rage and hurt you would feel towards the man who killed everyone you know and caused you so much pain and suffering. Immaculee, on the other hand, knew that forgiving was healing, and that holding so much pain and resentment towards the man would only bring her more pain and suffering.

She desired to heal, let go of the pain, and find peace with the situation, which meant forgiving him for what he had done. It takes a lot of guts to do this, but I truly believe Immaculee is on to something. You are only ever hurting yourself if you hold in everything that anyone has ever done to hurt you. Holding on to any pain or hurt will have an impact on all of your relationships, including your relationship with yourself.

It's Time to Take Action – Forgive Someone

I'm not suggesting you go out of your way to actively forgive someone for something they've done in the past. Contacting someone you haven't spoken to in years may feel strange. What you can do, however, is write down any past resentment or hurt that you believe you are still harboring.

Make a note of it on a piece of paper, along with a message to the person involved. Write as much or as little as you want, letting out all your frustrations and emotions in a letter format. Finally, simply write, "I forgive you." Read the letter all the way through, then rip it up and throw it away or burn it; this is a statement that will help you let go and truly forgive.

Take note of how you feel in the days following this, and you'll realize how effective it can be.

Last Thoughts

And with that, we have arrived at the end of our journey!

I hope, above all, that you found value in these pages and that you enjoyed reading this book as much as I did writing it. Self-discovery and development of any kind can be frightening and daunting, as well as very isolating if you don't know where you're going or what you're doing, but I hope this book can serve as a guide to help you find your way and make the changes you want to make in your life.

Relationships are such an important part of life, and it would be amazing to see how much of a difference the methods and information you've just read make. There are endless benefits to increasing your charisma and confidence, and as the saying goes, it's not what you know in life that matters, but who you know, and you know you've got the skills to bring these amazing relationships to life. Who knows what opportunities await you now?